American Catholics and Vietnam

American Catholics and Vietnam

edited by

THOMAS E. QUIGLEY

WILLIAM B. EERDMANS PUBLISHING COMPANY
GRAND RAPIDS, MICHIGAN

Introduction

While the pages that follow indeed bear what is called eloquent testimony to the anguish and passionate concern of certain American Catholics in the face of the Vietnam war, the book as a whole has an essentially more modest purpose.

It is not properly a state of the question for there is no single issue being reported on. Neither the morality of the Vietnam war — an issue debatable only within the code that weighs the possible carnage of a Kobe invasion against the actuality of a Hiroshima — nor the response made to that war by the American Catholic community is treated with systematic thoroughness.

It is, rather, a small voice joined with many others — in protest. It is what we, and the authors gathered here, can do after all the acceptable methods of registering dissent have been used up — speaking, signing petitions, picketing and politicking.

Others have done more, out of deeper conviction perhaps, certainly out of greater willingness to face unpleasant consequences. To them, especially to our brothers Dan and Phil Berrigan, we dedicate this small effort.

Special thanks are due *Ave Maria, Christian Century* and *Commonweal* for permission to reprint the Haas and Novak articles, to Gabe Huck for initiating with me this quest for a Catholic response, to Joseph Caulfield and Mary Lou Suhor for generous application of their uncommon skills and to Catherine who managed ever to encourage what often seemed to her a terribly devious form of witness.

— T.E.Q.

Contents

Biographical Notes

BLESSED ARE CERTAIN OF THE PEACEMAKERS
The Reverend Gerard S. Sloyan

Father Sloyan is professor of New Testament Studies at Temple University. Prior to assuming his present post he served as professor and head of the Department of Religious Education at The Catholic University of America, Washington, D.C., for approximately ten years. Father Sloyan has served as president of the National Liturgical Conference and of the Society of Catholic College Teachers of Sacred Doctrine. He is on the Board of Directors of the Institute of Judaeo-Christian Studies and the Editorial Board of *Religious Education* magazine. A specialist in doctrinal theology and catechetics, his books include *Nothing of Yesterday Preaches: Homilies for Contemporaries; Three Persons in One God;* and *To Hear the Word of God.*

A PEACEMAKING CHURCH
The Reverend Daniel C. Maguire

Father Maguire, whose specialty is Christian ethics, has been assistant professor in the Department of Religious Education at The Catholic University of America, Washington, D.C., since 1966. His writings include an essay, "War and the Christian Conscience," in *The Paradox of Religious Secularity;* a chapter on magisterium and morality in *Absolutes in Moral Theology,* edited by the Rev. Charles E. Curran; and articles in *Commonweal, Cross Currents,* and *The Living Light.* Father Maguire studied at St. Charles Seminary and in Rome for six years at the Gregorian University. He has taught at Villanova University and at St. Mary's Seminary, Baltimore, Maryland.

CATHOLIC EDUCATION, AND WAR AND PEACE
Mary Perkins Ryan

Mrs. John Julian Ryan is the author of numerous translations, articles and books, mainly on liturgical and catechetical topics, including the controversial *Are Parochial Schools the Answer?* Her latest book, co-authored with her husband, is *Love and Sexuality* (Holt, 1967). Mrs. Ryan has served as executive editor of *The Living Light,* a Christian education review published by the National Center of the Confraternity of Christian Doctrine, since its founding in 1964. The Ryans live in New Hampshire with their five boys, aged 13 to 25.

RENEWING THE CHURCH IN A NATION AT WAR

Daniel J. Callahan

A native of Washington, D.C., Daniel Callahan is executive editor of *Commonweal* — a weekly review of public affairs, literature, and the arts. He was educated at Yale and Georgetown and received his Ph.D. from Harvard, where he was a teaching Fellow for four years. He received the Catholic Institute of the Press award in 1964, and has authored several books, including *Generation of the Third Eye, Honesty in the Church,* and *The Mind of the Catholic Layman.*

CHRISTIAN EDUCATION AND THE
BROTHERHOOD OF MAN

Joan Bel Geddes Ulanov

Mrs. Ulanov is a consultant with the United Nations Children's Fund (UNICEF) and author of *Small World, A History of Baby Care from the Stone Age to the Spock Age* (Macmillan). Born in California, daughter of artist Norman Bel Geddes and sister of actress Barbara Bel Geddes, she is a graduate of Columbia University and mother of three children. With her husband, Barry, Mrs. Ulanov translated *The Last Essays of Georges Bernanos* (Regnery) and has in preparation a series of history books for elementary school children. She is a member of the Authors' Guild and President of the St. Thomas More Society in New York City.

THE CHURCHES AND CONSCRIPTION

Philip J. Scharper

Mr. Scharper, editor-in-chief of the publishing house of Sheed and Ward, is well known in intellectual circles through his articles and book reviews in leading magazines, as well as through his lectures at national conferences and on college campuses. His experience in working with members of diverse faiths in the United States led to his going to Rome in 1964 to act as a consultant on the Vatican Council Committee formulating Schema XIII, The Church in the Modern World, and again in 1967 to serve on the Vatican Secretariat for promoting Christian Unity. Mr. Scharper has made frequent radio and TV appearances and has written numerous television scripts on ecumenical themes. He has accompanied TV crews to Switzerland, Holland, Germany, England, and France to film programs on the World Council of Churches, Communism and Christianity, and a History of Man. He is chairman of the Board of the non-sectarian Religious Education Association of the United States and Canada, a trustee of the John XXIII Institute and on the Board of Directors of the National Conference of Christians and Jews, and of the Bishops Commission for Ecumenical Affairs.

DRAFT BOARD THEOLOGY

Michael J. Novak

Mr. Novak is chairman of the Common Humanities Seminar of the New Experimental Campus, State University of New York, in Old Westbury, Long Island. Through books and articles he has received international attention and acclaim. Mr. Novak spent the month of August, 1967, in Vietnam, studying the presidential election and his reports appeared in *The National Catholic Reporter.* His books include *A New Generation, The Open Church, Belief and Unbelief, A Time to Build,* and a novel, *The Tiber Was Silver.* A graduate of Stonehill College, Mr. Novak also studied abroad and at Harvard, where he was a Kent Fellow. The senior class at Stanford twice elected him one of the three most influential professors on campus.

CATHOLICISM, POWER AND VIETNAMESE SUFFERING

James W. Douglass

Mr. Douglass is assistant professor of religion at the University of Hawaii. During the Second Vatican Council he served as theological consultant to several British and American bishops on questions of war and peace in *The Constitution on the Church in the Modern World.* His book, *The Non-Violent Cross,* will be published by Macmillan in September. Mr. Douglass has taught at Bellarmine College in Louisville, Kentucky, and has written for *Commonweal, The Christian Century, Cross Currents, Continuum* and *Worldview.*

THE BISHOPS AND NEGOTIATION NOW

Thomas Francis Ritt

Long active in the Civil Rights and the American Peace movements, Mr. Ritt was the East Coast coordinator of Negotiation

Now, the national committee for a political settlement of the war in Vietnam. He has been national director of the Catholic Council on Civil Liberties and executive director of the New Jersey Democratic Council. For more than five years Mr. Ritt has been a featured commentator and producer for Pacifica Radio. His articles have appeared in a variety of national magazines and he is currently writing and narrating a series on "The Social Teachings of the Catholic Church" which he hopes to expand into a book. A recent lecture tour took him to campuses and colleges in thirteen states.

THE CATHOLIC PRESS AND VIETNAM
John Gerard Deedy, Jr.

A native of Worcester, Massachusetts, Mr. Deedy is currently managing editor of *Commonweal* magazine. For eight years he edited the *Catholic Free Press* in Worcester and for an equal time the *Pittsburgh Catholic,* before assuming his present post. Prior to that he served as correspondent with the *Boston Post* and *Boston Globe,* as well as on the editorial staff of the *Worcester Telegram.* He is co-author of *The Religious Press in America* and *Eyes on the Modern World.* Mr. Deedy studied at Holy Cross College in Worcester and at the Institut du Pantheon in Paris.

WAR IN THE PARISH
The Reverend William F. Nerin

Ordained in 1951 at Kenrick Seminary in St. Louis for the Diocese of Oklahoma City and Tulsa, Father Nerin has been a pastor for almost fourteen years. He is presently assigned to the experimental Community of John XXIII, and is a member of the Board of Directors of the Liturgical Conference. He received his master's degree in Family Life and Education at Columbia University's Teachers College and has been active in the Christian Family Movement, the Young Christian Movement, and the Newman Apostolate.

NO LONGER ALONE: THE CATHOLIC PEACE MOVEMENT
James H. Forest

Mr. Forest is national secretary of the Catholic Peace Fellowship and former managing editor of *The Catholic Worker* and *Libera-*

tion magazine. He is at present on the Executive Board for the Central Committee for Conscientious Objection and Associate Director of Interfaith Action for the Fellowship of Reconciliation. With Tom Cornell, he co-edited an anthology entitled *A Penny a Copy: Readings from the Catholic Worker.* Mr. Forest attended Long Beach State College in California and the New School for Social Research in New York City. He is a frequent contributor to newspapers and periodicals on subjects related to peace.

THE EUROPEAN CHURCH AND THE WAR

Gary MacEoin

Author, linguist, lawyer and newsman, Mr. MacEoin has published ten books while working as a journalist for the past thirty years on both sides of the Atlantic. A weekly syndicated column on world affairs for Catholic newspapers in the United States and Canada has taken him to some sixty countries in Europe, Asia, Africa, and North and South America. He is fluent in four languages and proficient in five others. Mr. MacEoin has taught at Columbia University and lectured at many other universities. He has represented the International Catholic Press Union at the United Nations and was chairman of the Inter-American Affairs Committee of the Overseas Press Club of America. A native of Ireland, he is an honorary citizen of Colombia and a citizen of the United States.

THE CHURCH IN VIETNAM

The Reverend Harry Haas

Father Haas, a Dutch priest-specialist in church dynamics and free-lance journalist, is at present assigned as chaplain to students at the College of Theology (Hogeschool Voor Theologie) in Heerlen, Netherlands. He has served in Ceylon, Germany, and the Netherlands in a specialized ministry to students, intellectuals, and youth workers from Asia, Africa, and Latin America. His special area of work and study is Southeast Asia, and he has participated in several missions to Vietnam. Father Haas has published widely and lectured on several continents. He is the author of *Christianity in the Asian Revolution* and *Catholics in Vietnam,* and co-author of *Christian Student Leadership for Asia.*

Foreword

GORDON ZAHN

Almost ten years ago a volume edited by William J. Nagle undertook an appraisal of "the state of the question" regarding Catholic teaching and attitudes on war *(Morality and Modern Warfare,* Helicon, 1960). Of the nine contributors to that collection of essays, this writer was the only professed pacifist, and it was largely out of this commitment that I was led to declare, "Given the nature and anti-Christian tone of modern war, including nuclear war; given the nature and at least non-Christian tone of the modern secular state and its rulers, I submit it is more fitting for the Christian to approach any actual or impending war under a general presumption of *injustice.* This at least would put the burden of proof upon the warring state and not, as is now the case, upon the individual with a troubled or doubtful conscience."

That suggestion sounds mild and cautious today, but it was a pretty "far-out" thesis to propose at the time. Certainly neither I nor my fellow contributors to the Nagle book could have dreamed that in a few short years the troublesome struggle in Southeast Asia would have blossomed into full-scale war, with America as major participant, and that Catholic priests and laymen would be playing a major part in a concerted opposition to the nation's war effort. Even more fantastic would have been the idea that so many of our more respected (and respectable!) Catholic journals would have adopted editorial positions denouncing the war as unjust and immoral. If it is still difficult for many, perhaps most, Catholics to recog-

15

nize the full dimensions of the significant shift in emphasis
that has taken place, the roster of the distinguished contributors
to this new volume should be enough to put the change in its
proper perspective. Reading what they have to say on the wide
range of subjects covered, one will have to confess that an
important corner has been turned. Perhaps it may be too
much to say — as Franziskus Stratmann, the great peace-
minded German Dominican theologian once put it to me —
that we are living "at the beginning of Church history"; nevertheless, the essays to be found within these covers will be
enough to show that American Catholicism has once again
learned to distinguish between Caesar and Christ, that it can
no longer be regarded as the automatic and unquestioning
handmaiden of the warmaking secular authority.

True, as several of the contributors note, the shift, significant
though it may be, has not put the pacifist (or, as some would
prefer, the peace-mongering) element of the American Church
into a majority or even dominant position. We remain a minority, but a rapidly growing minority. As such we are being
listened to with a greater measure of serious respect than ever
before. Except for occasional and particularly dramatic statements or actions — draft-card burning and the like — Catholic
pacifists are now far less likely to be dismissed as some kind
of lunatic fringe even by those who heartily disagree with us
and our arguments.

Although it is clear that not all the contributors to this
volume share my pacifist commitment, it is important that
we have this up-dated appraisal of the state of the question.
This is particularly so in that the question no longer revolves
around the morality or immorality of *nuclear* war, but, rather,
it has broadened to include all forms of modern warfare and
even carries the suggestion that those carefully defined and
elaborated formulations of the just war may never have been
relevant to the actuality of war. That the "entirely new attitude"
toward war and the evaluation of war called for by the Fathers
of the Second Vatican Council may require little more than
closing doors and stuffing loopholes that should never have been

permitted to open in the first place, is a proposition that demands the most favorable consideration. Not too long ago it was a proposition that, in the eyes of many, smacked of heresy.

A combination of many things has brought us to this new starting point. There was good Pope John, of course, and the Council he called into being. There were the progressive developments in military weaponry and tactics and the emergence at the same time of a new theology that stressed love and community, both of which taken together could not fail to force attention to the essential and ever more inescapable contradiction between the spirit of war and the spirit of Christianity. Finally, and perhaps most immediate and crucial of all, there was Vietnam.

In the providence of God it has often happened that good has come out of evil, not so much in the cause-effect relationship rejected in the evil tree and good fruit figure of Scripture but, rather, by shocking the evildoer into the full awareness of what he has done. This process, I think, has been started at least among American Catholics. We have suddenly found ourselves exposed to a wave of public denunciation in most of the other world capitals, and this has been traumatic to us who have been accustomed to seeing ourselves in the role of generous benefactor serving the cause of human dignity and freedom. The Paris walls bearing the legend, "US = SS"; the young German writer's declaration that Lidice and Oradour are today villages in Vietnam — no matter how we may try to close our eyes and ears to these things, they remain to trouble our national soul.

Thus the truly astonishing shift of Catholic opinion. To the extent that it represents a turning against legitimate authority, it is an almost unprecedented shift, at least in modern history. This volume serves as both an illustration and an exposition of that shift. Yet, I cannot help feeling (and this implies no criticism of the eminent contributors) that the picture which emerges is one of a change that is both too little and too late.

"Too little" if only because there are none included here who could be regarded as official spokesmen for the Church establishment. This would not be too significant were it not for the unchallengeable fact that their absence really does reflect a substantial unwillingness or inability to see and accept the facts that are set forth in these essays. Whether it be ignorance or indifference or, as is far more likely, nothing more than a compulsive dedication to a kind of overly cautious prudence, it has led to what amounts to a betrayal or surrender of the Christian message — necessarily and always a *prophetic* message in an un-Christian world! — by the very ones who hold the gravest and most direct responsibility for perpetuating and spreading that message.

This is a harsh thing to say, but what point is there for the bishops of the world to take a strong stand in support of the rights of the individual conscience and to urge that governments make due provision for conscientious objection when the overwhelming majority of American bishops finds it impossible to speak out against the religious discrimination against Catholics and others in the conscription laws of their own nation? Nor can we reconcile the high-sounding phrases of the Vatican Council's re-affirmation of traditional Church teachings in the matter of the freedom and supremacy of the individual's religious commitment with the position of the American cardinal who responds to an appeal that he support the right of the selective conscientious objector by saying, "I could never assume leadership in telling young men here or elsewhere that the war in Vietnam is unjust and *if they sincerely believed this that they should not serve.*"

The emphasis is, of course, mine, but it is not unfair or distorted. This same prelate was later to say of the hundreds of young men being called into military service that "probably most of those drafted are of the same mind, but they go through with it." This is moral bankruptcy indeed. If these men *are* of "the same mind" as the would-be conscientious objector (i.e. that the war is unjust and immoral), "going through with it" amounts to nothing less than what theologians have defined as formal sin — but this possibility escapes this august churchman completely. Some readers of this volume may feel that Thomas

Ritt is too easily impressed by the fact that a few American bishops were willing to identify themselves with so modest a program as Negotiation Now. Nevertheless, the fact remains that this innocuous level of criticism represents the highwater mark of episcopal disapproval of a war that has stirred open opposition on the part of prominent Catholic spokesmen in other nations.

But even if all these essays had been authored by top-ranking members of the American episcopate, they would be "too late" in the sense that the time for dominant focus upon moral principles and theological disputation has long since passed. Argument has given way to action. To a generation that has moved from the stage of detached scholarly discussion to dissent and beyond that to experiments in actual resistance, abstract assessments of the relevance of centuries-old "just war" teachings or approving quotations from clearly (and probably intentionally) ambiguous papal and conciliar statements seem less than adequate to the pressing demands of the moment. Courageous and deeply dedicated young men are already in prison; others are awaiting trial; still others are starting on the paths of resistance that will probably bring them, too, to the awful moment of decision when they must choose between jeopardizing their freedom and future or violating their consciences. For the rest of us to sit back and debate the application of the writings of medieval philosophers and theologians to the horrors we are perpetrating on innocent people thousands of miles away is a cruel waste of time and intellectual effort. Even if we do come up with some answer that succeeds in building a bridge of theological continuity across the centuries that separate us from St. Augustine and St. Thomas Aquinas, it will be an empty success if, in the meantime, men like "the Boston Five" will have been jailed for advising young men to be true to their consciences and others, like the Berrigans, will share that fate because they felt they had to turn to "the symbol of the act" to give more urgent and direct expression to their rejection of an immoral war.

This, again, is not a criticism of those who have contributed

to this volume; for these shortcomings are, unfortunately, a true
reflection of the state of the question. While other men, most
of them acting without the inspiration and strengths supposedly
furnished by our religious wellsprings, have found sufficient
inspiration somewhere else to recognize evil and moral strength
enough to reject and resist that evil, American Catholics still
have not been able to free themselves from the notion that open
opposition to one's own nation's war policies and objectives is
a kind of treason — spiritual as well as political.

The war is one problem, the draft is another — and it will
be with us after the war is brought to an end. I am gratified
that several of the contributors have raised the issue of selective
conscientious objection and have questioned the principle
behind the involuntary recruitment of young men to serve in
wars of ever more doubtful morality. Michael Novak's incisive
commentary on "draft board theology" raises necessary questions, but it does not go far enough. We should protest a structure that puts draft board personnel in a position where they
can *and do* function as theological "experts," passing judgment
upon the validity or consistency of the religious convictions of
others. For example, a young man I have counselled was called
before his draft board for a preliminary hearing on his application for conscientious objector status. The three Catholic
members dismissed his carefully reasoned arguments — arguments supported by generous citations from papal and conciliar
documents, the writings of theologians, statements from leading
(European) bishops, and the like — with the flat assertion that
a Catholic cannot hold the position he presented, that, if he
thought he could, it could only be because he did not know his
own religion and had not "read all the red print in the Bible"!

The incredible stupidity such a comment displays is not the
real point at issue. That state authority, represented ultimately
in men like these, is able to arrogate unto itself the power to
decide upon the "correctness" of any individual's religious
beliefs and applications of those beliefs — this is the issue we
must confront. If the First Amendment guarantees of religious
freedom mean anything at all, the Selective Service *as it actually*

operates violates constitutional principle, yet, as so many have learned to their despair, there are no effective procedures for overruling this system or challenging its final decisions.

It should be no surprise, then, that many sincere believers — happily including a growing number of Catholics — have reached the conclusion that conscription itself is wrong and must be rejected. Sometimes their break is limited to a personal refusal to cooperate further; sometimes it takes the form of more direct interferences with the System itself and its operations. Thus, however one may question the effectiveness of the tactics they chose, I would insist that the Berrigans and their Baltimore colleagues deserve support and admiration for the essential point they were trying to make.

Even if we are not yet prepared to join or actively support the "Resistance" movement as it has taken shape in our country, all of us as Catholic Christians should be ready and willing to understand and respect those who have concluded that anything short of resistance is rendering service to the wrong master. It is incumbent upon us to insist that the rights of dissent are respected; to make sure that a fair hearing be given to all, whether by a draft board vis-à-vis its dissenting registrants or by judge and jury deliberating some act of civil disobedience.

It would be well, too, to pursue the issues raised by Philip Scharper, especially that portion of his essay relating to the question of sanctuary. Certainly there is much in our own religious tradition that should put Catholics in the forefront of those insisting that the right of sanctuary be reaffirmed and respected by the secular authority. But here again our official spiritual leaders do not appear in the best possible light. While other Christian leaders have defended and offered sanctuary, most of ours have remained silent. Not too long ago, I joined in a discussion of the issue in which the participants, all Catholic, priests as well as laymen, simply took it for granted (a) that it would be all but impossible to find a Catholic Church which would provide sanctuary (even, be it noted, to the Catholic deprived of the CO-classification through the religious discrimination already discussed); (b) that if there were any chance at all of finding even one, it would probably be one of the "inner core" parishes where pastors are perforce more permissive or, in large part the effect of their own pastoral experiences, more "radical"; and (c) that under no circumstances could one approach a bishop or chancery officials for approval before (or after!) the event.

As a self-judgment, this is a shocking indictment of failure on the part of the institutional Church. But it is one that is fully justified in the light of the prevailing concern for prudence and institutional security that has locked the Church into fixed patterns of near total conformity and compliance.

To fulfill our mission as Christians, we must break with these patterns. Each of us must be prepared to go as far as we can to support those who choose to follow their consciences, even if we might not agree with the substance or tactics involved. We must do everything possible to build an enlightened opinion and spread understanding. Draft board officials should be approached by committees of priests and informed laymen on behalf of young Catholics who reject military service; even more important, perhaps similar efforts should be made to persuade the *parents* of such young men that such a decision should be a source of pride (in having a son who is willing to risk so much to be true to his conscience) and not an occasion for efforts to "pressure" him into doing what he thinks is morally wrong and, failing in this (as has happened in far too many cases), casting him out of the family circle for bringing "shame" upon them by his refusal to conform.

What I am saying, I guess, is that we need much more emphasis upon action even at the sacrifice of some of the philosophical and theological niceties to which we Catholics are so addicted. Perhaps if this were to happen, this volume might be the last such effort at principle-oriented persuasion American Catholics will need before they can mount a really effective opposition to war and all that makes for war. If so, we might even dare to hope that a few years hence still another state of the question may be published in which the trembling beginnings represented in the Nagle book and developed in such a promising manner here will finally have reached fulfillment in an American Catholic community that will have discovered and accepted the full implications of the Christian message of love for all men as brothers and the promise of peace to follow.

The Catholic Church and War Today

1. Blessed Are Certain of the Peacemakers

GERARD S. SLOYAN

THE ROMAN CATHOLIC, LIKE ANY CHRISTIAN, IS IN principle deeply committed to peace. If he were asked whether Jesus of Nazareth was a peaceful man he would immediately reply in the affirmative. To the further question whether the follower of Christ is expected to pursue peace with all his strength, he would say that he has the obligation. Yet the paradox exists. Most Catholics are of the opinion that the injunction to peace is a matter of avoiding strife in domestic, business, and other personal contacts, whereas they tend to think that strenuous efforts to bring war to an end ill befits the Christian. The supposition of many Catholics is that serious engagement in peacemaking at a national or international level is a sign of disloyalty to one's country and indeed a vice opposed to the virtue of patriotism. Peacemaking, in other words, is a fitting activity at a personal level but not at a political level.

We should, perhaps, confine our remarks to the Catholics of the United States, for those who reside in lands that have been the scene of wars — as this country has not been since 1864 — are much more earnestly committed to efforts at political peacemaking than are we. When Pope Paul VI came to the United States as a United Nations' guest in 1965 there was apprehension in the hearts of many U. S. Catholics that he would "enter politics" by asking this country to pull out of the Vietnam war. At that time the Vietnam war was as popular in this country as it ever became. Even today, one has the impression that it was always a much more popular conflict with the

Catholics of this country than with this country's citizens generally.

When we speak of a war as being in any sense "popular" with Christians, we have identified not a paradox but a genuine impossibility in the life of the Church. The whole question deserves some examination.

The Savior described his peace as a peace that the world cannot give. The ultimate source of the peace he gives us is his Father. From him Jesus receives all that the Father has. Much of this he is able to transmit to us. Peace is a gift from Jesus Christ to men. However, although peace is heavenly in its origins, it has to do with the harmony or discord men experience on earth. The peace Christ gives is not an ethereal or transcendent peace unrelated to life in the world. The context of peace or the absence of peace may be personal or familial, tribal or civic, national or international. Whatever the case, it is very much a matter of earth, though it is a gift from on high. We shall be examining shortly what the terms of the gift of peace are.

Peace for the ancient Israelite was the gift of his God Yahweh. Yahweh, or "the Lord," was at peace and he willed that his people should be at peace. In the early desert days he was conceived to be a conquering God of armies. He was likewise thought to be an avenging God, a God of strife in the sense that he cracked the heads of those who did not submit to his sway. But this is the way he was conceived in imagery, not the way he was. The Old Testament speaks of God as he was known to a particular, ancient people. The only way they could know him was through their history as a people and through the interpretation put on it by their great figures filled with religious insight, the patriarchs and prophets. These men thought of God as being at peace in himself, but achieving peace for others by way of conquest in battle.

The brutal conduct of ancient Israel is readily enough explained to anyone who is at home in cultural history and the *mores* of the world of four and three thousand years ago. There was much savagery abroad in those days. The people of Israel were part of the ancient world and did not escape its savagery. The Old Testament is the record of a people over many centuries — a hot-blooded, demonstrative, Oriental people who had a great conception of God and who came to be purified in their moral life, both personal and political, as they let the implications of their concept of God affect their conduct. Often enough the Israelites did not see what the effect of the holiness of Yahweh on their conduct should be. Often, too, they saw but resisted the logic of what they saw. They did not let his person have the effect on them he clearly wanted it to have, and this resistance the Bible calls "sin." War and violence are reprobated in the Bible, if by Bible we understand both Testaments of Scripture. The moral purification of the lives of the men of the Bible was a continuing matter. It was brought to completion only with the teaching of Jesus and his gospel of peace. Still, the Old Testament is not primarily a record of holy wars or violence in Yahweh's name. It is before all else a call to holiness and peace, a peace of which God is the author.

It is possible to quote Old Testament passages at length in an attempt to establish that war is or is not a defensible practice, but such proof-text exchange is in the long run time lost. What the Hebrew Scriptures convey is a spirit, a trend, a drift, and that drift is unmistakably in the direction of peace. Peace is first something in men's hearts and then it is something between neighbors, whether Jew and Jew or Jew and non-Jew, between any human grouping or faction. Peace for the Hebrew is the result of the personal will of Yahweh in man's regard. It is his benevolence or well-wishing whereby he both orders all to go well with us and sees to it that it will happen so.

The New Testament attributes to Jesus, at least by implication, the Isaian title *Sar Shalom,* "Prince of Peace." Jesus is undoubtedly a man of peace even though he does not hesitate on one occasion to say he has come to bring not peace but the sword. He divides, it is true; he separates households, setting daughter against mother and mother against daughter, among others, but only in order to reconcile and heal and fuse into one. The peace that Jesus brings is not cheaply bought. It has a price and a high one. He does not espouse living in harmony despite unreconcilable ideals. His is a peace achieved after much reflection, a peace with honor. The peace of Christ is the possession of those who accept the will of the Father.

The spirit of Christ is not a spirit of selfishness, avarice or greed, but rather one of openheartedness and openhandedness. Only in such a spirit is peace available to his followers. Those who seek their own interests cannot be peaceful men. Jesus, in his earthly days, was anything but a bellicose man. He described himself as meek. In speech he was gentle, if forceful, at all times. The gospel record does of course reveal that Jesus was no stranger to wrath in a just cause. His ejection of the traders from the temple is a classic case, and he attacked his hypocritical opponents in bitter terms. He protested strongly against an unjustified blow on the face during his brief captivity, and he addressed himself to Herod and Pilate in tones of cold contempt. The peaceful Jesus was not an apathetic man; he took action, strong and vigorous action, in the cause of righteousness.

Jesus was peaceful in an active way, working to bring about the conditions of his Father's peace in the kingdom. His emotions were pent up at certain times and released at other times. He never failed to speak in the cause of right. He always acted for what was right even though at times, as in his passion, that action was a submission. St. Paul tells us that he went to his death willingly for our sakes out of obedience to the will of the Father. He himself said that he had the power to lay down his life and to take it up again. He went to his death in the way he did, however, because in a very real sense he had no choice. He was the victim in those dark hours of a violence from which he shrank and which he could not humanly overcome. Despite our knowledge of his previous election to give his life freely for the sake of his brothers, we know that the hour of darkness overtook him with the inexorability of that blind cruelty which overtakes any helpless victim.

All of Jesus' utterances were in the way of peace, of intelligent, courageous action to bring about the possibility of openness to this gift of God. In the interests of peace Jesus asks men to cast all bitterness out of their hearts. He requires that they give and love and serve and share. If this advice is followed it leads to the end of quarreling and depredation and murderous destruction. In a word, it brings an end to war, whether that unlovely expression of human hatred is carried out on the battlefield or in the civil arena or in the church or in the home. Wars declared and undeclared, spoken and unspoken, fought with or without instruments of carnage, are brought to an end by the full acceptance of Jesus' spirit of peace.

The notion of the Church as the great protagonist of peace on a social as well as on an individual scale came slowly, if it came at all. The development was made in halting and painful stages. In the first five centuries of the Church's life, Christians were encouraged not to become soldiers. They were even forbidden by some writers to serve in armies, frequently because of something extrinsic to the conduct of war itself. An oath of fealty to the emperor was required which conceived of him in terms of deity. Hence military service was outlawed because of its connotations of idolatry. Again, army service was written against vigorously because of the evil associations possible in that life. There is no strong and clear voice from a Christian writer, however, that forbids participation in armed conflict for the precise reason that the Savior forbade it. Tertullian in the late second and early third centuries remarked that Christians were found everywhere. It is well known that they were found in the Roman army, and even that Christianity achieved some of its spread through this means.

The church fathers were silent on the subject of war for the most part until the time of Augustine. He is for all practical purposes the author of the Christian theory of the "just war," a theory he devised to meet the pressing problem of his own time, the barbarian threat to the Empire. Augustine contended that because of the Christian's charity, no disciple of Christ should kill in self-defense, since he should not love life or property more than God or neighbor. He went on to say that in order to maintain peace, rulers have the right, at times the duty, to make war, and their subjects have the duty to obey when the command is not clearly opposed to a law of God. Augustine proposed one legitimate reason for making war, namely, the defense of peace against its serious rupture. But even a just war must be waged in a spirit of mercy for the defeated and with peaceful intent. Further, war must be circumscribed by three considerations: its purpose, its authority, and its conduct. Despite the fact, however, that Augustine argued this theory, he never seemed to have satisfied himself as to the full compatibility of war with Christian charity.

Various theologians developed Augustine's argument, though not very far. Among them were St. Thomas Aquinas and the sixteenth and seventeenth century theologians Vittoria and Suarez. The Augustinian argumentation has continued down to our own time, at least through the papacy of Pope Pius XII, who even in the age of atomic, bacteriological, and chemical warfare argued in 1949 that "there are some goods of such importance for the human community that their defense against an unjust aggression is without doubt fully justified" (*AAS*, 41, 13).

The next theoretical step after Augustine was the idea of the holy war, and its practical manifestation was the Crusader. It cannot be denied that the Crusades were preached as a vindication of the honor of God and Christ against the infidel Turk and the Jew. A facile association was made between the Christian cause in reclaiming the holy places and the fate of the kingdom of God. Rape, burning and looting, frequently against helpless villages along the way to Palestine, were the bitter fruit of this misbegotten zeal for the gospel. The relationship between Christians and Jews and between Christians and Muslims was worsened almost beyond repair in the period of the Crusades.

The notion that war-making in itself did not involve one in serious guilt was supported by the brevity of life in the Middle Ages, and by the notion that, compared to eternal life, life in this world was unreal. There was a conviction abroad that there was little harm in snuffing out a man's life because he would shortly be in the hands of a just judge anyway, where he could get started on the serious business of eternal life or eternal death.

It must be acknowledged that a churchwide commitment to peace in the Christian order did not come until the seventeenth century, with its various streams of Protestant pietism. It is true that a number of medieval sects described as heretical at the time had a more than ordinary interest in evangelical peace.

It was, however, left to various groups of evangelical brethren in Germany, the Low Countries, and England to identify themselves wholeheartedly with active resistance to war. Notable among these in the English-speaking world was George Fox's Society of Friends, who were led by an "inner light" to do the works of peace. The larger church bodies, Roman Catholic, Evangelical, and Reformed (Lutheran and Calvinist), seemed too enamored of the idea of the Christian prince, defender of the faith and of the alliance between throne and altar, to take the prophetic stance.

In our time it is a commonplace and not by any means a slander to observe that the higher clergy of all the major churches have blessed weapons, been active in support of armies, and devised theological rationales to establish why "God is on our side." They have not tended to be sympathetic to the peacemaking tradition that goes back to the great Christian saints, Catholic and Protestant, and ultimately to Jesus himself. Some have even given evidence that they think peacemaking to be the work not so much of moral weaklings as of the deluded, the naive, those who will not come to terms with the spirit of lawlessness abroad in the world. There can be no question that there is such a mystery of iniquity, that demonic powers exist which are opposed to God and Christ. Paul taught that such a principle of evil exists and is being restrained, even if not perfectly, until the end of time. It is further true that patriotism is a virtue for the Christian when it does not veer by excess toward a chauvinistic spirit of narrow nationalism.

Pope Pius XII has rightly said that in an era familiar with

weapons of mass destruction, failure to defend human liberties would give "free field in international relations to brutal violence and lack of conscience" (*AAS,* 45 [1953], 748). There can be no question that situations arise in the modern period in which all hope of averting war seems vain. Unjust attacks by nation upon nation have been a regular happening since the beginning of this century. Wars of self-defense marked by some hope of success and entered into as a last resort cannot be thought of as illegal. They may, in certain circumstances, be thought of as obligatory. However, the case of the nation unjustly attacked and menaced in its vital rights is not the case we speak of here. We are more concerned with the thoughtless assumption that a certain war is right because one's country happens to be engaged in it. Too frequently the proposal is dismissed out of hand that grievances should be examined in conferences, however tedious and even humiliating, before hostilities are declared. Too frequently ultimatums are issued saying that the offenses of neighbor nations are to be punished, lost lands are to be recovered, expansion into roomier territory is to be sanctioned, for the reason that a nation has needs and aspirations that cannot be fulfilled within its own territory.

Churchmen should be in the forefront of every action for peace. As a matter of fact, however, taking all of Christendom into account over the last six decades, churchmen have a record of having been almost solidly in support of wars. Many have not hesitated to associate themselves with the war machines of their own nations. The papacy has a reasonably good record, but only since it was stripped of its temporal holdings in 1870. Certain Protestant groups, notably the World Council of Churches and the National Council of Churches of Christ in the U.S.A., have made bolder declarations than anything stemming from official Roman Catholic sources other than the papacy. We must ask why this is so.

The most evident reason — aside from the possible failure of Roman Catholic churchmen to be lovers of peace in the gospel sense — is that international Communism has been identified as an anti-religious force since the Russian Revolution of 1917 and even the European uprisings of 1848. Second only to the possessing classes, Roman Catholics have been major victims of the Communist techniques of spoliation and disenfranchisement. Thus an identification has been made between the work of Satan and the Communist cause everywhere. The same mentality that finds conspiracy everywhere, whether of international Jewry, Freemasonry, or anti-Catholicism in its various forms, has been quick to recognize the conspiratorial hand of Marxism or Stalinism everywhere. Little or no account has been taken of the aspirations of the people in Communist countries to get enough to eat or to throw off the shackles of feudal oppression. Often these bonds have been made fast by Christian sovereigns, colonial exploiters, or native landowners. Christians in this country generally have not cared to know why Communist regimes have been welcome alternatives to governments in power. The formula is much too attractive that equates Communist leadership with Satanic power. It is a clear case of black and white for the Christian, and he chooses white. Consequently, the great bulk of Christians, and Roman Catholics in particular, are of a mentality which holds that opposition to world Communism comprises a holy war in the strict sense. There is much talk of enslavement of peoples and of the rights of small nations to self-determination. In fact, however, the fate of the Church as an institution is often the chief thing at issue, without any special inclination to discover whether self-determination might not result in a Communist regime. The people might indeed choose one in an attempt to overcome the evils they have experienced under Christian, Buddhist, or Muslim control.

It has all too easily been supposed that active work for peace ends inevitably in laying down one's arms, following which workers' states or peoples' states may take over. One thing that the Christian must get clear, which by and large he does not have clear, is that the clamor for peace from many in the Marxist sphere is quite genuine. The early means to achieve this peace are deplorable. They include what is thought to be the necessity of taking freedoms from workers so that ultimately

the proletariat or greatest number of people may enjoy the
fullest freedom. There are serious flaws in the economics of
Marxism, whether pure or developed, but in concept a state of
free workers is looked forward to, not a state of the enslaved.
The only meaningful response to the appeal Communism has is
an economic and political system that will bring more freedom
to the greatest number sooner. With the exception of a few
scattered governments and governmental efforts that have received Catholic sanction, the normal Catholic response to active
peacemaking is an almost pathological fear of being duped by
the Communist world.

The popes are our sole men of concern, practically speaking.
We have arrived at a handy formula whereby we must praise
all they do or say in this line, but no other Catholic person is
free to work for peace without suffering almost immediate
opprobrium. Catholic pacifists are few, but they are known to
be men and women of courage. Their activities in demonstrating
against war — for example, in framing petitions against the
Vietnam war — are looked on with suspicion by the great bulk
of United States Catholics. Yet, these men and women are
being faithful to the gospel of Christ as they understand it, in a
way at least as courageous as that of any frontline soldiers.
Their entire concern is to see that there are no frontline soldiers.
They want our finest young men out of the trenches, out of the
rice paddies, more than anything else. For their efforts they are
reviled. We cling to the conviction that the only honorable
way to extricate oneself from a war is to slaughter one's way
out or be slaughtered; we fear every peace but one of total
victory as a dishonorable peace. We will not believe the Savior
when he tells us we must be lovers of peace, understood as a
gift of God to which we lay ourselves open.

Many of our contemporaries who are neither pacifists nor
Marxists have nonetheless been strongly opposed to the engagement of the U.S. in the Vietnam war. Certain of these persons
are not opposed to all wars but they have opposed this one.
Ranged opposite them are other thoughtful people who think
most wars savage and senseless but this one justified because

of its presumably vast implications. How is a Christian to take his stand, both on war in general and on the Vietnam war?

First of all, he cannot forget what he knows about history and government, hunger and tyranny. One is not required to become politically unsophisticated just because he has deep religious convictions. No, retaining all he knows about political reality and the enduring presence of evil, the Christian is by definition constrained to deplore the fact and the theory of war. It should be expected that he will be in the forefront of all attempts to achieve a lasting peace. But the first and most serious proof of this will be his concern to bring to a halt any war still in progress. He must hate war as he hates sin because it is the fruit of sin and leads to sin. He must, in a word, be a man of peace by doing the works of peace—and this he will find as unpopular in any age as other works in the life of Christian virtue.

2. A Peacemaking Church

Daniel C. Maguire

THERE IS CONSIDERED OPTIMISM IN THE TITLE: IT implies that the Church *will* have a meaningful role in the complex dynamics of peacemaking in the modern world. The optimism, I confess, is tinged with hesitation. I recall the evening that Paul Lehmann of Union Theological Seminary was guest speaker at the dedication of some church educational buildings. After a tour of the splendid buildings, Dr. Lehmann spoke and startled not a few as he asked: "Do you know what you have created here? A resplendent mausoleum. It stands here incandescent in the glow of its own irrelevance as the dynamics of the time rush to pass it by." Despite this beginning, Lehmann managed to work to a hopeful conclusion that the Church might not be buffeted and bypassed, but could actually help shape the revolutionary forces of the day. Perhaps we, too, can hope that the Church's voice will not be a bleating in the wilderness but in some way will be a source of the word that gives life and peace.

At any rate, we must begin with the hope that our creatively pacific influence in the human community is not utterly conditioned by our past performance. The Church's record in the face of war is not a cause for celebration. Rather it turns us to the poignant reminder of Karl Rahner: "The Church is a sinful Church; that is a truth of faith, not just a fact of her primitive experience. And it is a shattering truth."

From the earliest times, Christians were divided on questions of war and peace. Some would serve in the army; some

39

would not. Pre-Constantinian literature was not so ambivalent as practice. A grand chorus of pacifistic utterances came from the pens of Justin, Athenagoras, Tertullian, Cyprian, Origen, Minucius, and Arnobius. Some would see in this the golden age of Christian pacifism. This is uncritical. It was a pacifism largely untested by war and colored by the defensive and apologetic needs of persecuted Christians who wanted to prove themselves no threat to the Empire. Legitimate conclusions from this period would appear to be these: (i) Christians brought from their encounter with Christ an unprecedented sensitivity to the horror of bloodshed and they enunciated its basic incompatibility with the gospel ideal. (ii) They did not hesitate to offer prophetic resistance to the power structures of the Empire in matters of conscience. Indeed, they became such a notable social force that the Emperor Decius was quoted as saying that he was less concerned over the news of the revolt of a rival emperor than by the election of a new bishop in Rome. (iii) Some witness to the peacefulness of Christ was given in frontier warring situations by requiring ministers of the sacraments to abstain from fighting.

When Constantine won the Empire under Christian auspices, Jesus became a Lord of War and Christians leapt from persecution to preferment. (Jesus, by the way, was militarily active at this time in the East where a bishop reports that in response to prayer, the Lord routed the Persians by sending a cloud of mosquitoes and gnats to tickle the trunks of the enemy's elephants and the nostrils of his horses. It was hardly a match for the Milvian bridge but it does show some versatility.) But suddenly a new Christian chorus was heard. The befriending sword was not about to be beaten into a plowshare. The sensitivity to military service so completely disappeared that by the time of Theodosius II only Christians were permitted to serve in the army. Intoxicating honors and subsidies were heaped upon the Church and the arrival of the eschaton was proclaimed. Since the Christian is called to prophetic tension, nothing could befit him less than satisfaction with the status quo.

But this precisely was the Constantinian mood. A new situation had brought a new morality.

Augustine's baptism of the just war theory has had sufficient notice. I emphasize two points only which have had a tragic and persistent resonance in Christian history. First, in order to ease the Christian warrior's pain at having to return evil for evil, Augustine, who would not allow a private citizen to kill even in self-defense, tended to blend the Old Testament idea of the God-inspired war with the idea that the power of the state comes from God. Thus a soldier preserves his innocence by the right order of obedience. This motion presaged the surrender of personal responsibility to government and recalled the grand illusion of the holy war.

Secondly, Augustine paints a picture of a warrior who goes to kill with love in his heart that is so unrealistic as to be macabre. "Love," he writes, "does not exclude wars of mercy waged by the good." Thus, the impossible but alluring vision of war as a conflict between the simply good and the simply bad. (Historian Roland Bainton mentions that a good case might be made even for the barbarians!)

Then, enter the barbarians — for whom violence was a way of life. Their religious consecration of violence was almost complete. It was unhappy destiny that the Church would complete it for them. Ineffectual gestures such as the Truce of God did not stay the mounting fever of violence that gripped the Western world. The violence that could not be subdued was diverted, and the Crusades were born. The sword became the instrument to establish the center of the kingdom of God in Jerusalem. One of the best public relations jobs in the history of the Church proceeded from the Council of Clermont, and Europe came ablaze with zeal for the salvific war. Indulgenced warriors were sent out to the slaughter and their weapons were blessed with liturgy so that those who wielded them in piety might crush their foes with vigor through Jesus Christ our Lord. Monastic perfection and the holy war were wed in the Knights Templar. Heaven was promised those who died in battle. And there was no effective protest among the hierarchy or the faithful. The intellectual strong men were not much disturbed either. Aquinas, in a classic example of theology's emphasizing the wrong questions, gave one question in the *Summa* to war and twenty-four long ones to angels.

In the just war theory (which traditionally has no rules for the other side since it presumes them utterly wrong) and in the spirit of the Crusades, we have the important elements of much subsequent Christian theory and practice. War is seen either as a crime or a crusade. This was the prevailing mind-set of the mellifluous Bernard and Zwingli, of Calvin and Suarez, of Luther and Francesco Vittoria. Wars, caused by a series of unprotested mistakes, continued. The great wars of the twentieth century found churchmen rallied around their respective flags. The just war theory worked nicely for both sides, assuring each that theirs was "a war of mercy waged by the good." Some resistance to the bombing of population centers appeared in the beginning of World War II but the dynamic of violence prevailed and there followed Coventry, Birmingham, Hamburg, Dresden, Hiroshima and Nagasaki. By the time of the atomic bombings the word target had come to include population center. And the churches were remarkably still! Since World War II the old Christendom versus Heathendom syndrome has reappeared without subtlety in the form of Democracy versus Communism. This phenomenon has been widely and perhaps sufficiently discussed.

And what are the prospects and potential of the Church today? To begin with, we must recognize that our historical Christian heritage in the matter of peace is not without debits. There lingers in our historically conditioned personalities a tendency to sacralize national policy in matters of war. A certain insensitivity to the horrors of war is a legacy with which we have not yet dispensed. The formation of a more sensitive ethos in this regard is a prime need of the Church.

Secondly, as we work to meet that need, we must forthwith rid ourselves of the outdated notion that initiative, teaching, and influence are reserved to the Church's hierarchical figures. Paternalistic magisterial figures may once have made sense;

today church leaders must serve to activate the resources of the entire ecclesial community. They must interpret their "authority" through its root word *augere*—they must seek to give increase. Bishops and popes should see it their principal duty to inspire initiative, to promote research, to preserve unity without stifling creativity, and when possible, to give sensitive utterance to the relevant experience of the Church.

Thirdly, person-to-person contact has always been the most effective teaching technique in the Church. It is this technique today that will most promote the cause of justice and peace — if Christians can be oriented to the mission of peace. However, let us not lose the realism of the ancient liturgy, which loved to couple the epithets "all-powerful and merciful" in addressing its Lord. It takes power for mercy to be operative, especially in mass society. Protestant groups, responsive as they are to issues of peace and justice, lose much of their impact because of their splintered image. Even the World Council of Churches feels more inclined to speak to its members than for them. Hopefully the Catholic Church will not lose all of its monolithicity! The power structure of a church with some organic, sociologically identifiable unity is needed to plead the cause of the *anawim* with the increasingly powerful power structures in society. Prophecy is not incompatible with power, and there are some devils abroad today that are not going to be cast out with prayer and fasting. I do not hesitate to say, for example, that if the Catholic Church were sufficiently concerned about the incompatibility of the present CO law of the United States and what is implicit in the CO doctrine of Vatican II, it could bring about a change in that law, quickly. We shall return to that presently. For the moment, suffice it to say that lobbying, pressure, power are in themselves morally neutral terms.

Finally, agencies must be erected in the Church to allow strong minority voices an officially Catholic platform from which to speak. The three cautious statements on the Vietnam war by the American bishops did not represent an important segment of the Catholic population, who were thereby left to plead their case "unofficially" in predictably receptive journals, and thus they lacked the important sociological power factor of institutional prestige. Agencies must be erected that will permit the layman and the theologian not just to communicate with the hierarchy, but allow them to communicate, as Catholic representatives, with the world.

It can be said that there are signs that Christian consciousness today is progressing toward a more critical and discerning realism. We have started to move from a quibbling ethics of war to a broader ethics of peace and this trend has found papal and conciliar expression. It is progress to have recognized that the casuistics of armed conflict do not deserve prime attention. Prime time belongs to the socio-cultural problems that breed despair and hostility. The war/peace problematic is now centered on the problems of poverty and exploitation and on the expanding inequality of power possession. We listen now to the voice of the Nigerian lawyer, 'Bola Ige, "Our basic demand is for a share of the power now concentrated in the hands of a minority of mankind." We focus a bit more honestly, too, on the pseudo-democratic forms that we encourage in the developing nations and upon the obsessive American "hang-up" that sees democracy as the only way to prosperity. We are even stumbling onto the idea in Vietnam and elsewhere that our battle is not primarily against an alternative form of revolution but against the realities that make revolution in some form absolutely essential. We are beginning to realize, too, that the national and racial *hubris* and sham of capitalistic and communistic endeavors in the third world insult and alienate beneficiaries and create a screaming need for prophecy on the part of the churches. We are perhaps ready to face the implications of facts such as the failure of the United Nations Conference on Trade and Development, which occurred chiefly because neither Communist nor Western nations were prepared to make the radical revisions of their economic policies necessary to meet the needs of the seventy-five third-world countries involved.

Fine. We realize a lot of things now. We are a bit less myopic. But the magisterial challenge that faces the churches is this: We must take our Christian experience of essential brotherhood and hope, find how it applies in a cynical world, and then pierce the insensitivity that holds back our dream. And at this point I have fear and trembling and pessimism. I am thinking mainly of the Catholic experience, which I know best. Let me put my pessimism in bold print.

(1) The task of peacemaking is a task of peace-teaching. It is a work of communications and we are poor at this. It is not only sad but significant that the communications decree of Vatican II was dubbed the weak sister of the documents. In the midst of multiplying media we show few signs of moving from ossified forms. Study of the possibilities here has no priority.

(2) Teaching is an outer-directed social activity. A sense of persons and their needs is essential. I see here another Catholic debit: a lack of social consciousness. We have not met such social questions as the abolition of slavery, civil rights, anti-semitism policies, or war with distinguished prophecy. A 1966 Gallup poll showed 54 percent of Catholics approving the U.S. policy on Vietnam as against 39 percent of Protestants. I read in this, aside from an immature dependence on the decisions of authority figures, a certain detachment from the problem, and I wondered whether much of that Catholic "opinion" could not have been filed under the No Opinion column.

I am afraid we are not about to bring to the peace issue the zeal we have displayed in fighting pornography. I am afraid there is a caricature of our myopic insensitivity in the German chaplains who accompanied Hitler's troops in the brutal invasion of Holland zealously warning the soldiers against the Dutch prostitutes. I'm afraid we'll hide from responsible citizenship by the use of evasive distinctions such as, "It's political not moral." I am afraid, in a word, that we do not love the world enough.

(3) The magisterium is in an important way a person-to-person operation, and we are losing persons. Not by apostasy or schism. Those terms referred to persons who took "church" seriously. The departures are not as dramatic as that of Charles Davis but implicit in them is a similar rationale: They feel the

spirit has gone out of the structures, or, more hippily put, the Church "is not where it's at."

(4) Catholics have moved from a small ghetto to a somewhat larger one and called it aggiornamento. The masses of our people still think parochially, and this is often supported, quite congruently, by the structure called parish. Even we liberals who feel *ouverte au monde* must be chastened to learn that 99 percent of the nation doesn't even read *The National Catholic Reporter*. Intra-tribal problems consume us. Confessional "hang-ups" — the contraception issue is an example — absorb us unduly, liberals and conservatives alike. Meanwhile bishops fiddle in dismay over liturgical excesses while the world burns with undirected revolutions and expanding inequities.

(5) Finally, in my pessimistic litany, the bishops. In a true sense it is not the bishops who worry me most. I think that in religious bodies we get the leadership we want and then ease our consciences by criticizing it. The bishops are not tyrants; their people are with them. If the percentage of popular support for the local ordinaries were publicized, any political office holder would be livid with envy. Most people are addicts of bourgeois comfort and their identification with supportive structures reaches their bone marrow.

Apposite to this, the remarks of Victor Ferkiss reviewing Dorothy Dohen's *Nationalism and American Catholicism:* "Why pick on the bishops? . . . since when do bureaucrats (even of the ecclesiastical variety) make the best prophets? Political and social leadership is the job of all of us. Why complain about being led astray by false shepherds when it is our duty — as Christians and as Americans — never to act like sheep?"

And now a bit of optimism.

(1) Even the rather haphazard type of witnessing for peace that has been going on has not been all futile. At least Prentiss Pemberton buoys us up by observing, "Most of the peace aims now being affirmed by our government were declared first not by Washington but by the critics of our policy."

(2) No matter what we have done, society persists in expecting something from us. Maybe the message of social

philosophy where a person is seen essentially as the counterpart of other persons has had an impact or given voice to a new reality. Maybe isolating individualism is in decline and men are open to meaningful expression of group consciousness. If so, we have an audience.

(3) Christianity gives us an international brotherhood, which if strengthened could speak louder than the bickering of the nations.

(4) The recent "intrusion" of the laity into the church might just move us into practical research into the multiple ways of exerting instructive and constructive influence in tech-nopolis. In advance here we exclude nothing: drama, arts, research teams and centers, political lobbying groups, civil disobedience (which is a going form of instruction) and public demonstrations. Maybe even the liturgy could become didactic again!

(5) There is still a great challenge open to bishops and popes and other religious authority figures. Human hearts still sing "Hail to the Chief." Our discontent with episcopal performance is not all negative rancor. It is also an anguished prayer and a broken hope. We would really like the bishops to show courageous Christian initiative, to move from an ethic of survival to an ethic of creativity. If the bishops move from their timid administrative ways to a leadership that is distinctively Christian and unafraid, their influence can be massive.

A renewed and truly magisterial Church, which is hierarchical and lay, organized and unorganized, institutional and interpersonal, which dresses "churchy" and goes "incog," ought to move quickly in certain areas.

First, we should recognize that revolution is not a prospect or a possibility but a fact of life. The deprived of the world are no longer disposed to live in a degrading accommodation with the growing inequality of wealth and power distribution. With or without us political and social revolution in varied forms shall take place. Since neither capitalism nor Communism as now in effect embodies the ideals of the Sermon on the Mount, Christians must be prepared for revolution. Since the Christian

Church also in its present realization falls short of the Christian ideal it too must be viewed with a revolutionary eye.

We must study the techniques of revolution, especially non-violent revolution, but we must not exclude the possibility of bloodshed. Existent revolutionaries of other persuasions should not be judged by their adherence to the Nicene Creed; we should not exclude in advance supporting them or recommending their support. Our God, remember, is a surprising God. As Andre Dumas has pointed out: "He does not preserve and maintain; he breaks through. He is called a living God, unlike dead idols or ideas, because he takes by surprise and reshapes the very things that idols neglect or confirm." We must brace ourselves for surprises if we would listen to this God.

Second, we cannot work for peace in the human family without a radical redeployment of our resources and personnel. To address the prime problem areas of peace, poverty, and race, and to avail ourselves of the signal opportunities in the field of adult education, we may have to divest ourselves of some of our choicest projects. For example, Catholic hospitals are not continuing for the reasons they were begun. Of necessity they are businesses today; only a tax-supported hospital can afford free care for the *anawim*. Furthermore, as good theology begins its inevitable trek to the secular campus, Catholic universities and colleges have soul-searching to do. Catholic grammar schools and high schools should be asked to justify their existence. The answers will vary with locale, but the questions must be asked. Some religious orders fought fires in the Middle Ages but they knew when to get out of the work; we are thus spared the phenomenon of the Catholic Fire Company, and of firemen who vow to extinguish blazes in poverty, chastity, and obedience.

Third, John Kennedy said: "War will exist until the distant day when the conscientious objector enjoys the same reputation and prestige the warrior does today." Today, in both church and state, it is the objector who must justify his position and not the warrior. Presently under fire is the U.S. Selective Service Act which requires an objector to oppose war "in any form." Although practice is not as oppressive as the law, the law is a bad one. It first of all imposes a bad system of ethics and deprives conscience of its discriminating role. It would be a comparable error to say that a person must approve of all divorces or none. The law also is counter to the dominant tradition of Christian bodies, which is not one of religious objection to war "in any form." I would reject the law on the same grounds that I reject an absolute pacifism, in that it negates the decisive ethical import of particular and varying circumstances, which at times could indicate war and at times prohibit it.

The majority report of the National Advisory Commission on Selective Service advised the President last year that "so-called selective pacifism is essentially a political question of support or nonsupport of a war and cannot be judged in terms of special moral imperatives." To allow the individual such a decision, they said, would be equivalent to "taking away the government's obligation of making it for him."

The error here is hardly less than fantastic. It perniciously separates the terms "moral" and "political"; these terms are distinguishable but not separable. Politics is concerned with human life, and whatever is concerned with human life has a moral dimension. A society that forbids a person to judge that a particular war is unjust and concedes him only the possibility of an unreal ethic that would ban all war without contextual analysis and differentiation infringes on the rights of man in an immoral fashion.

I grant you that this moral problem has its political side; I grant you that a new law could be abused, and could make for many practical problems. After granting this I remain aghast at our neglect of the consciences of thousands of young men, who know as much about the war as many congressmen, who would allow a presumption in favor of governmental authority if there were not serious doubts as to its "credibility," and whose consciences do not enjoy the respect of the law. In their fall meeting in 1966 our bishops expressed worry about the infringement of freedom of conscience in welfare agencies which were dispensing information on contraception. Their case here was dubious at

best. Their moral indignation would have been better directed
to this question. With transcendental blandness their subsequent statements on peace have continued to ignore this problem. On this issue, once again, the lack of alertness of the
hierarchy reflects perfectly the concomitant sluggishness of the
conscience of the laity.

Fourth, the magisterial Church must look searchingly at the
continuing tragedy of Vietnam and become a prophetic presence
on the national scene. The Church should be the matrix of
honest, non-partisan discussion of the war. Churchmen should
work to create in their people an ethical sensitivity to war/
peace issues and to jar Christian consciences free of their
Constantinian moorings. Christians must learn that Christianity
cannot depart the flesh of society's needs and happenings. If it
departs, it is guilty of a docetist betrayal of Emmanuel, the
incarnate "God with us." Knowledgeability in matters of national policy is essential to Christian life. Detachment here
is apostasy.

If the voice of John Courtney Murray had been heard in
1959, the Vietnamese situation would not have deteriorated as it
did. "As a moral problem," he wrote, "war is not simply or
even primarily a problem for the generals, the State Department,
the technologists, the international lawyers. Here, if anywhere,
'the People shall judge.' This is their responsibility, to be dis-
charged before the shooting starts, by an active concern with
the moral direction of national policy. My impression is that
this duty in social morality is being badly neglected in America
at the moment."

After Murray wrote those words, that war developed and
expanded and communication between government and citizens
progressively diminished. This is the way of war. The "credibility gap" was not a Johnsonian creation. In war time governments traditionally behave in a totalitarian fashion. Under the
rubric of necessarily "classified information," national policy is
lifted from the redeeming and corrective influence of democratic
processes and discussions. Factors that could decelerate the
meshings of the military machine are kept from public view.

War ceases to be seen as a tragic breakdown of international politics, and military considerations smother the development of creative diplomatic alternatives. Dissent is seen as disloyalty, as openness and flexibility disappear.

The Johnson Administration merely acted out an established historical syndrome. The nation, however, has become less tolerant of these maneuverings. Our society is proving its ability to get to the facts and social morality is awakening. People will no longer, for example, accept an Administration-claimed readiness to enter "unconditional discussion" when many conditions and vacillations are a matter of public record. History might well record that it was Johnson's fate to preside over the demise of the old way of governments at war. Sadly, and indeed tragically, it seems that an administration that cannot assess the signs of the times is destined to go down railing against developments that it does not understand. Leadership is never more seriously indicted than when leaders not only cannot lead the forces of history but cannot even follow them.

The Church must encourage this hopeful development and help to give it shape. Christian consciences must never be nationalized. Christians should try to bring honesty and objectivity to the great debates. It might be well to admit now that the war in Vietnam has actually done some good. Maybe it is good that the charge of paper tiger has been dropped. Maybe our effort has reenforced nationalism in Southeast Asia; our presence may have fostered the development of the various national groupings that have sprouted in that part of the world. Maybe nuclear proliferation has been somewhat contained in nations that have now been convinced that we will honor our nuclear commitments. Maybe. At least we must honestly explore these possibilities as we point out the drastic disadvantage of that and any similar war.

Christians critical of the war have a problem of catechesis in dealing with those who are instinctively disinclined to question national policy in time of war. Critics often fall into a cyclic dialogue with themselves. Being right without being communicative has the effect of being wrong. The man in the street does not like to waste money, does not like sham, does not like projects that do more harm than good. We have not yet convinced him that this is the case with war. Our catechesis is poor.

Governments will never become ingenious in the pursuit of peace as long as citizens are insensitive to the tragedy of war. The Church's massive task is to help to create this sensitivity. The Church has sinned against peace in the past. Its hour of redeeming grace may be at hand.

3. Catholic Education, and War and Peace

MARY PERKINS RYAN

PEACE DEFINED AS "THE TRANQUILITY OF ORDER" (St. Augustine) is the kind of peace that Catholics have generally been brought up to cherish. But, as John McKenzie for instance pointed out recently in an article in *The Living Light,* this idea of peace is a negative one: the absence of noise, disturbance, enemies. It is all too like the concept of *pax romana,* about which Tacitus, putting the sentiment into the mouth of a British chieftain resisting the Roman invasion, said bitterly, "They make a desert and call it peace." And so the majority of Catholics are willing to tolerate the deserts of our city ghettos so long as "order" is not disturbed. They are willing to tolerate the desert that the United States is creating in Vietnam to insure the absence of enemies and the establishment of "order" in Southeast Asia.

But the peace that Christians are supposed to be making, peace in the biblical sense, *shalom,* "by contrast has a very positive content. One meaning of the verb related to this noun is 'to finish' or 'to complete'; it is the word used to designate the payment of a debt. It is a state of 'accomplished' well-being." Thus to be a peacemaker, the Christian must be struggling against whatever forces in himself and in his society are destroying, diminishing, or threatening human well-being; he must be fostering whatever promotes healing, reconciliation, freedom, dignity, creativity, development of persons in society. In other words, he must be cooperating with Christ's own work: "I am come that they may have life, life in abundance."

The Christian, therefore, must be willing and able to disturb the kind of order which makes or preserves the "peace" of a desert, and to do so responsibly, in ways best calculated to bring about a greater degree of true peace, *shalom*. He must be willing to be, as William Stringfellow puts it, a "dissenter" in every society, for the sake of human well-being, to prepare for and build up the kingdom which will be the fullness of life in union with one another and God "all in all."

Thus Christians need to cultivate all the elements of the virtue of prudence, that is, the cultivated power to make wise decisions both as to what should be done and as to how best to go about doing it. These elements, as analyzed by St. Thomas, are: to learn the facts, to determine the underlying values and issues involved, to reason logically, to proceed step by step, to make sure that all the factors have been taken into account, to use the advice of experts and one's own inventiveness and resourcefulness in arriving at a final decision. In other words, the Christian should equip himself, as the Constitution on the Church Today puts it, "to serve the men of the modern world ever more generously and effectively," putting prudence to work in wise action, in the service of love. He should equip himself to be an informed, intelligent and active member of present-day society, which can only survive if it has more of such citizens taking part in decision-making at every level. We are experiencing today the unhappy results of the passivity about social structures and government that produced the climate engendering the riots in city ghettos and the war in Vietnam. The only hope for the future is for Christians to unite with all men of good will to create a different climate, a climate of informed and active concern for *shalom*.

To meet today's needs, general education must train people in evaluating, appreciating, and decision-making; in social and international awareness, and the methodologies to implement effective and creative thinking and acting, by individuals and by groups; happily, the best trends in modern education are in this direction. In the same way Catholic religious education must change its main thrust away from giving a training in obedience and passivity and towards helping people to grow in awareness, in responsible freedom, in the power to make wise decisions and to act on them, in the service of love.

The best trends in the "new" catechetics are in this direction. But they are meeting with some outright opposition — for example, the "Concerned Parents" and others' reactions to the third-grade text of the *Word and Worship* series as being "too human," and as presenting Martin Luther King as a Christian hero — and a great deal of puzzled incomprehension. It may be useful, therefore, for readers concerned with adult education — their own or others' — as well as parents and teachers, to point out some of the reasons for the "old" thrust of Catholic education and also the basic sources of the new one. For if we are all to "get with it" as rapidly and effectively as possible, we need to understand the presuppositions behind the order-keeping Catholic mentality in which we were all brought up, as opposed to the positive "peacemaking" one.

Catholics, and Protestants too, are only just beginning to realize the Christian vocation as one of creative dissent in any society. During many centuries, one might even say since the peace of Constantine, the Church has been placed in or has assumed the position of an order-keeper for civil society. The Church has, generally speaking, been part of "the Establishment," with the Christian religion serving the function of keeping its adherents from rebelling against the injustices of the socio-economic status quo as well as fortifying them to bear with the other "breaking-points" of human life — suffering, frustration, death. Of course there have been exceptions, when the institutional Church has come out strongly on the side of the poor and the oppressed, and innumerable instances when individuals or groups within the Church have fought for change against the Establishment. But generally speaking, the Church authorities have been on the side of the status quo, particularly in recent times. This is just as true of the Catholic Church in the United States as of any Protestant Church. Although it began as the church of immigrant groups and was suspected of being the agent of a "foreign power," the Catholic Church today is as interwoven with the socio-economic Establishment, and as identified with its white middle-class values, as is any other "respectable" Christian Church.

Many complicated factors, obviously, have been responsible for the Church's taking such a stance in different societies, from the peace of Constantine to our own times. But one of these, and one most important in the American Catholic situation, has been its view of its own mission as consisting in *teaching* as many people as possible what they must believe and must do or not do in order to save their souls, *sanctifying* them by providing them with the necessary means of salvation, Mass and the sacraments, and *governing* them so that they will believe and behave in accordance with what the authorities have decided are the requirements of Christian faith in given concrete situations.

This view of the Church's mission to mankind is in turn dependent on a particular view of "salvation" — the view presented, for instance, in the Baltimore Catechism, which has little in common with the idea of salvation as the achievement of *shalom*. The impression given by the Baltimore Catechism is that God is only concerned with "souls," not whole human persons, and with whether or not they die in "the state of grace," understood as a kind of quantitative reality conferred by Baptism and restored or increased by the other sacraments, and always in danger of being lost by "mortal sin," the latter understood as the intentional transgression of a law. In this view, it does not matter very much what a Catholic does with his life so long as he stays out of "mortal sin" and frequents the sacraments. He will achieve the purpose of his existence, salvation, that is, getting to heaven, if he believes and behaves as he is told. Obedience becomes a prime virtue, for the adult as well as the child; decision-making is not encouraged; and passivity seems preferable, because safer, than action. Obviously, this is a vastly oversimplified version of the presentation of the Faith common until quite recently. Yet I do not think that it is an unfair one, as to its general thrust.

Moreover, to this way of looking at things, the quality of human life in any society does not matter very much. What matters is that it be made as easy as possible for people to have the truths of faith explained to them, so that they will believe what they should, to be told what is sinful (and how sinful) so as to avoid mortal sin, and to make use of the "means of grace." Thus any kind of orderly society that guarantees the "free exercise of religion" is to be upheld, still more one that publicly acknowledges God, upholds Christian moral standards and generally favors the practice of religion as an accepted and respected aspect of its life. For in such a society it is presumably easier for people to save their souls, in the above sense, than it would be, for example, in a Communist one.

All this explains, at least in part, why Catholics generally are so apathetic about the treatment of minority groups; as they understand it, their only duty to the unfortunates of society is to perform "works of mercy" for them, not to try to *change* the social structures that seem to be assuring energetic and upward-bound citizens, at least, "all this and heaven too" — the opportunity to improve their own socio-economic status *and* to save their souls. It also explains why they are generally willing uncritically to support our government's efforts to fight "godless Communism" anywhere in the world. For Communism threatens both their middle-class values, which they have, also uncritically, accepted as Christian ones, and their chance for eternal salvation, since the Church might no longer freely teach and administer the sacraments. Thus Catholics easily see the role of the United States as a messianic one: to save as much of the world as possible from Communism and to help its peoples establish the American way of life, in which a large number of citizens, if not all, can have as it were the best of both worlds.

In trying to help Christian adults to understand and accept the role of peacemakers, with all that this implies, it seems to me essential to help them realize that the Church is calling on them to assume this role because the Holy Spirit is leading it to a deeper understanding of salvation and of the mission of the Church and of Christians. The Council's document on the

Church in the Modern World, for example, ends with the strong statement:

> Mindful of the Lord's saying: "By this will all men know that you are my disciples, if you have love for one another" (Jn. 13:35), Christians cannot yearn for anything more ardently than to serve the men of the modern world ever more generously and effectively. Therefore, holding faithfully to the Gospel and benefiting from its resources, and united with every man who loves and practices justice, Christians have shouldered a gigantic task demanding fulfillment in this world. Concerning this task they must give a reckoning to Him who will judge every man on the last day.
>
> Not everyone who cries, "Lord, Lord," will enter into the kingdom of heaven, but those who do the Father's will and take a strong grip on the work at hand. Now, the Father wills that in all men we recognize Christ our brother and love Him effectively in word and in deed. By thus giving witness to the truth, we will share with others the mystery of the heavenly Father's love. As a consequence, men throughout the world will be roused to a lively hope — the gift of the Spirit — that they will finally be caught up in peace and utter happiness in that fatherland radiant with the splendor of the Lord.

This statement in turn implies the whole re-orientation taking place in dogmatic and moral theology: that sin is essentially the refusal to love and to act lovingly; that grace is God's offer of the ability to go out of ourselves in love, a gift He offers to all men; that the salvation which He desires for all men is the fullness of human personal and communal life and love "beyond what the heart of man can conceive" in union with Him and one another; that our human task is to help one another towards this salvation, this *shalom;* that the particular task of the Christian and the Church is, in carrying out this task, to proclaim the faith that, in Christ, God is with us and for us in this task, and the hope that it will ultimately and transcendently be achieved.

It is only in the light of this "new" view of the purpose of human life and of the Christian's task in the world, it seems to me, that Catholics will generally be aroused to a real concern about social or international issues; that they can be brought seriously to consider the position of the Christian pacifist, or the serious application of an updated "just war" theory, the many questions connected with the armaments race, or the relinquishment of the United States' role as world savior from Communism in favor of the apparently riskier course of much greater support of the U.N. We have to remove the theological blocks that have become psychological ones from our own minds and those of our fellow Catholics and make our own the vision of a real implementation of the great commandments of love of God and neighbor after Christ's example, before we can wholeheartedly engage in the work of peacemaking. This is an educational task in which we all can and must share, by word and by example, wherever and however we can carry it out.

4. Renewing the Church in a Nation at War

DANIEL J. CALLAHAN

IT WOULD BE EXCEEDINGLY PLEASANT TO SAY TWO things at the outset: that the Vietnam war has posed a major crisis of conscience for American Catholics, and that the on-going renewal within the Church has given Catholics a new sensitivity to war and destruction. Neither of these things may be said. They are simply not true. To be sure, one can easily find Catholics to sign petitions urging negotiation or withdrawal, just as one can find Catholic editorials and articles condemning the war. But it does not take long to discover that more or less the same small group of people sign most of the petitions and write most of the anti-war editorials and articles. Now and then a new name appears, even the name of a bishop; it is an occasion of note, however, when this happens.

The overwhelming picture presented by American Catholicism is of a passive, unprotesting, faintly chauvinistic herd, satisfied to go along with the Administration. In this respect, American Catholics are much like the rest of the population, and if (according to some polls) they are somewhat more favorable toward the war than other groups, the difference is not all that striking. There is a small group on the left that would like to see the United States leave Vietnam immediately, and a small group on the right that would still like to see a total war waged for the sake of a quick, total victory. In the middle, there is just a large, thick lump, on the whole ready to go along with whatever the government happens to think best. It is not an inspiring picture.

A naive outside observer might, though, find it a surprising picture. After all, Pope Paul VI has repeatedly called for peace in Vietnam; the Second Vatican Council had many strong exhortations, did it not, about the Church's responsibility for humanity, justice and peace; there has been a powerful ferment since the Council, calling many traditional Catholic attitudes into question and reforming many traditional institutions. How can it be that on the issue of the Vietnam war, Catholics have been so indistinguishable from everyone else? How can it be that Catholics have responded to the war as if nothing whatever has been happening within their Church during the past decade? How can there be such a discrepancy between all the new Catholic talk about "the world" and "human dignity," and the patent fact that the mass of Catholics suddenly became deaf and blind in the face of the suffering of the Vietnamese people?

These are embarrassing questions and, if they are also "naive" questions, one must ask why on both counts. They are embarrassing because they point once again to the age-old difference between Catholic rhetoric and Catholic reality. In a Church that has for so long laid heavy stress on saying the right things (with extraordinary care being taken to phrase doctrinal pronouncements with precision), there has been a corresponding tendency to act as if reality is changed by words rather than actions. As long as Catholics *say* they are for peace, they seem to think they have done their bit for peace; the rest is in the hands of God and the Administration. Catholics do not of course act this way when their immediate institutional interests are at stake; there is no shortage of people or schemes or actions when it comes to supporting the parochial school system, for instance. But as soon as the issues become more general — more human than Christian and more Christian than Roman Catholic — words are left to do the work of intelligence and action. The Vietnam war provides a perfect example. No doubt Catholics would prefer peace in Vietnam. No doubt they are as distressed as any other group about the cost of the war and the fact that Americans are still being killed (it is not so clear whether there is much distress that Vietnamese, north and south, are being killed). But it should be inescapably clear that this kind of good will changes nothing. In fact, it can even be harmful. When everyone is in favor of "peace" (and who isn't?), and the public consensus accepts war as the way to peace, then a general call for peace merely sustains the war consensus. The Johnson Administration has had a splendid ally in the Catholic people and their episcopal leaders—the Catholics call for "peace" but helpfully allow the Administration to define what the word is to mean in Vietnam.

There is another sense in which the questions are also embarrassing. For they imply that there should be some direct link between internal reform in the Church and the Church's actions in the world. And this is an implication, it should be confessed, that Catholic reformers have themselves accepted and fostered. The working assumption of Pope John XXIII was that the first step the Church should take to make itself credible to the world was to clean its own house; and it was an assumption gladly taken up by most articulate reformers in the Church. The trouble, perhaps we are beginning to see, is that there is no necessary link at all. It is quite possible to make many extensive, even dramatic changes within the Church and yet, in the end, have as little impact on the world as ever. This is why questions that are embarrassing can also be naive. For, in the face of the evidence, is it not naive to expect automatic transfers of energy, imagination, and zeal from one domain (the inner) to another (the outer)? Being a good parent does not necessarily make one a better citizen. Being a good parish activist does not necessarily lead a person to become a good political actionist. Being a good exegete of Scripture does not directly lead to being a good analyst of guerrilla wars of liberation. Creating community in the Church will not necessarily help the creation of community in the world. The Church, though, has expected that this would happen.

One needs to get to the roots of this naiveté, to see what has gone wrong and what needs to be done about it. Let us look at the main issues of Catholic renewal. The most important thing to notice is that almost every step taken toward renewal has been one that brings the Church more into the mainstream of American *mores*. So far as I can determine, most non-Catholics approve heartily of Catholic liturgical reform, greater lay participation, episcopal collegiality, free speech in the Church, reform of the religious orders, an affirmation of "the world" and a blessing of "secularity," just as they clap when the Church shows signs of changing its mind on contraception and clerical celibacy. However much all these issues may be hotly controversial within the Church, they are hardly controversial at all outside. To most non-Catholics, the changes in Roman Catholicism since Vatican II have not demonstrated that a new prophetic force is afoot in the world but only that the Church is finally getting some sense in its head; and better late than never. At most, Catholics are no longer looked upon as odd and medieval; they are getting to be like everyone else.

I do not say this by any means to make fun of all these reforms in the Church. I wanted and want them as much as anyone else. I only want to point out that, in the context of the Church's relationship to society and politics, they are reforms which have no cutting edge at all. They cut, but only within the Church; outside they merely open doors and make Catholics more at one with the main line of American values. Far from making the Church more prophetic, they only make it more congenial. But am I not neglecting the Church's stand on racial justice and the need, to take another instance, for rich nations to help poor nations? Surely these stands have a cutting edge? Well, not really, since even here there is a fairly strong verbal consensus in this country in favor of racial justice and helping poor nations. Since every elected Presidential Administration for the past two decades has stood for these values, it is hardly daring for Catholics to support them.

Where, then, could there be a cutting edge? On the Vietnam war, the knife of reform would cut very deeply if Catholics exercised their Christian right to call the political morality of the Administration into serious question. It would cut even more deeply if they decided, as a Christian community, that the war is unjust and refused to support it. Unlike changes in the liturgy and religious orders, this kind of change in Catholic stance could make Catholics very unpopular, not congenial at all.

While one could easily and correctly observe that such a change in Catholic political thinking is as much called for in the Council documents as is a change in, say, liturgical thinking, one should also observe *which* changes Catholics have seized upon and which they have slighted. What one sees is selectivity. And it seems to have turned out that those changes that American Catholics as a whole have most enthusiastically selected are just those changes that bring Catholics closer to the thinking of Main Street America. To put it another way, Catholics have been rapid to embrace those reforms that will make them much like everyone else and slow to embrace those reforms that would make them "different." To American Catholics bent on taking the final step into full acculturation, the Council was a gift from heaven, a delightful marriage of theology and social aspiration. Needless to say, the Church's teaching on the duty of Catholics to condemn unjust wars (particularly the Vietnam war) could sunder that marriage; hence, it is not surprising that affluent, socially acceptable Catholics have made little of it. All reforms are equally worthy, but some reforms have fewer harmful social consequences than others. Catholics have shown a sure instinct in deciding which would have the most pleasant consequences and which might be social disasters.

Since what I have just said may sound offensively cynical, let me add some extenuating circumstances that need to be taken account of to get a more rounded perspective. One of these circumstances has to do with what many sociologists have referred to as the trend toward "privatization" in contemporary life. By this they mean a tendency among people living in massive, technocratic, bureaucratic societies to seek their psychological salvation and sense of meaning in the private rather than the public sphere. Since it is unhappily true that the individual and small groups find it hard both to identify with the ends and purposes of large industrial nations and to make any difference in the life of these nations, they tend to turn inward to private satisfactions and small group activities. One place they may turn is to the church and synagogue. Here they can find purposes and meaning and here they have a chance of influencing the course of ecclesiastical events. I would suggest that one reason Catholics have been so much stronger in working for internal reform in the Church rather than external reform of society is that they, too, are caught up in the trend toward privatization. It may be difficult and frustrating for a layman to succeed in changing his parish, but it may be far easier to do this than to change secular society. Here is another sense, then, in which the Council was a gift from heaven for many Catholics: the Council, with its call for internal renewal, provided a kind of theological rationale for what they felt driven to anyway — the turning of their energies toward that which seemed to be manageable.

Still another circumstance is undoubtedly the lingering legacy of doubts concerning the patriotism and loyalty of American Catholics. The non-Catholic may no longer, since John F. Kennedy, entertain these doubts, but many Catholics have probably not been able to forget that they once did. The tradition of American Catholic super-patriotism dies slowly. One should recollect that it was nursed by a long theological tradition of subservience to "legitimate" political authority, justifiable immigrant nervousness over many decades, and the enthusiasm of the immigrant for his newfound land. Relevant also is the lack of any tradition of coalition between Catholic and non-Catholic social and political critics. The last decade has seen signs that such a coalition may now be possible, but it is still not the case that Catholic and non-Catholic reformers are naturally drawn together. Catholics have been far more successful integrating themselves into the mainstream of American conformism than into the mainstream of American reform.

Another extenuating circumstance I would describe as a matter of temperament. Theologically, Catholics are taught to be careful and patient, weighing all "responsible" viewpoints and remaining deferential to those in authority. The revolutionary viewpoint — whether theologically or politically — gains little support from Catholic tradition. Reform is fine, but it must be a wise, prudent, balanced reform, taking infinite care not to destroy any long-cherished values in the process. As the reforms in the Church of late have demonstrated, one can change much in the Church if one is willing to wait forever, to avoid emotional outbursts and to play a careful, cagey political game. That at least is what bishops and solemn theologians keep telling the hotheads. The same temperamental bias appears when it is a question of reforming society. Doubtless the bishops and many Catholics genuinely want racial justice in America. But they want it slowly, gradually and peacefully, with as little strife as possible. Catholics, it is pleasing to say, are not always dumb. Their trouble these days is likely to be the opposite: they are too smart, too taken up with the complexity of life, whether in Church or in society. They want to wait, to unravel the problems slowly and cautiously; to make no leaps that the evidence will not bear; to go nowhere until they have carefully looked over the terrain.

It is hard to complain about this kind of temperament, for it is one way of trying to be rational. But something very disastrous can happen when an issue like the Vietnam war comes along. It is a complex war, hard to understand, hard to predict, and hard to make decisions about. Just the kind of war, in short, guaranteed to make anyone trying to act rationally hesitate. No one can really say what would happen if (a) the American troops were suddenly withdrawn, or (b) North Vietnam was systematically obliterated, or (c) a policy of small escalations accompanied by periodic peace feelers was continued indefinitely. One would be a fool to make predictions. It is much simpler, and on the face of it more rational, just to keep saying it is a "complex" war raising "complex" issues and to ask, imploringly, for more time to think about it all. This, I would guess, is the stance of most American Catholics. They are confused, hesitant, and uncertain.

In the meantime, as American Catholics rationally mull over the alternatives in the war, the war goes on. For all the "rationality" of saying the war is complex, it overlooks one thing: while the rest of us mill around, turning the problem over patiently from all angles, thousands of people are being killed and two nations are being ruined. Our cautious temperament, fearful of making a mistake, helps kill as many people now as does an obvious blunder. Our patient, careful worrying is of no use to the people of Vietnam, however useful it may be to the Administration.

When one compares the fantastic energy that has gone into implementing the liturgical changes with the energy that Catholics have put into ending the war, one can only be ashamed for the Church. When one sees the money and imagination that have been lavished upon the Catholic schools, and how little of anything other than silence has been spent to end the war, the sense of shame grows. When one thinks that the Catholic Church is meant to be a light to the world, one can only ask: where is this light? It is certainly not shining in Southeast Asia. While the bombs were falling, while the search and kill ("reconnaissance in force") missions were bombing the countryside, and the people were dying, American Catholics were renewing the Church. Yes, there are excuses and explanations and extenuating circumstances one can bring up to relieve Catholics of an excessively guilty conscience; it is not easy to renew the Church and it leaves little energy for much else. And we may just succeed in renewing the Church. It will be an acceptable Church, clean and fresh and modern. We will be praised by our fellow citizens for our good sense, for throwing out a dead past. It is just possible, however, that in our preoccupation with our own housecleaning we will manage to miss the whole point of it all. And what is that point? To make Christianity mean something, say something and do something. The Vietnam war was our first major test since the Council: a test to see whether we are anything but pompous spouters of empty words. We have so far failed that test, and there is not much time left.

5. Christian Education and the Brotherhood of Man

JOAN BEL GEDDES ULANOV

"YOUR VOCATION IS TO MAKE BROTHERS NOT ONLY of some but of all men. . . . The United Nations is the great school where everyone becomes a pupil and also a teacher in the art of building peace." This is the "message for all mankind" that Pope Paul delivered to mankind's representatives at the United Nations on October 4, 1965.

The Pope was inspired and inspiring. The tall glass building glowed with faith, hope, and love as he cried, "No more war, war never again!" How enthusiastically everyone nodded when he said: "Relations between peoples should be regulated by reason, justice, law, negotiation, not by force or violence, not by war, fear or deceit."

The world was a cheerful place that day. Since then its mood has plunged from euphoria to chronic fear and bewilderment. The most powerful nation on earth has plunged itself ever deeper into a long, costly, increasingly destructive struggle against one half of one of the smallest, weakest nations in the world: Goliath's strength is challenged by David's slingshots. The violence in Vietnam, witnessed daily on TV by the impressionable and the disturbed, speaks louder than words like "negotiation" and "brotherhood" and "reason." Other countries imitate our example and wonder why we deplore their flouting of international agreements. The gap in living standards between the wealthy and the poor nations grows steadily wider, creating mounting bitterness and hostility as people in desperate need of jobs, decent housing, education, and medical help are doomed to squalor and despair because the money that could supply these things is spent on destroying, not on building. People think it normal for governments to spend incredible sums of money to kill or threaten people (it is "necessary" for "security"!) when they "cannot afford" to spend equivalent sums to help people. Not even one percent of the gross national product of the prosperous nations is spent on behalf of the underdeveloped nations. The United Nations Children's Fund (UNICEF) struggles to provide for the urgent needs of the world's undernourished and ill and uneducated children (more than half the children in the world) on an *annual* budget equal to what the world's governments spend every two hours on armaments. Yet the Bible, which Christians supposedly believe, asks, "If someone has worldly goods and sees that his brother is in need, and fails to show him compassion, how does the love of God live in him?" Pope Paul's highly praised message did not consist of vague generalities. He said,

> If you wish to be brothers, let the weapons fall from your hands. You cannot love while holding offensive arms. Those armaments, especially those terrible arms which modern science has given you, long before they produce victims and ruins, nourish bad feelings, create nightmares, distrust and somber resolves; they demand enormous expenditures; they obstruct projects of union and useful collaboration; they falsify the very psychology of peoples. . . . Divert to the benefit of the developing countries at least a part of the savings which could be realized by reducing armaments.

Although everyone applauded, only one government, Iran, acted upon this suggestion during the following year and diverted one day's armament budget to the anti-illiteracy work of UNESCO. One day's offering out of 365 is pathetically little — but it is more than any "Christian" nation diverted from *de*struction to *con*struction.

"Peace is not built solely by means of politics and the balance of forces and interests," said Pope Paul to the UN. "It is constructed with the mind, with ideas, with works of peace."

Ideas and works must supplement each other for either to

have maximum value. For two thousand years Christians have been affirming the importance of love and peace, but even those who have been wholly consistent in what they believed and said have not always *acted* loving and peaceful. In trying to convince people, they have often used methods that defeated their purpose. Good will is not, alas, enough to teach successfully; intelligence, imagination, ingenuity, psychological health and insight, technical skills, and energetic and appropriate activities are also necessary. Emotional guidance is as vital as spiritual training, and practice is as important as theory.

Catholics have always believed that the purpose of education is to develop character as well as to impart information — most of them, if they had to choose between virtue and knowledge, would opt for virtue. Many Catholic elementary school teachers emphasize good conduct more than intellectual excellence. But why should there be any conflict? Using one's mind to the peak of its ability is an important kind of good conduct, and there is no reason why intellectual and aesthetic standards should have to be low in order to keep moral standards high. In fact, mediocrity accepted in any area of life is apt to contaminate other areas.

In spite of the avowed desire to develop holiness in their pupils, the tactics used by many well-meaning teachers are more apt to produce smug, lazy, narrow-minded accepters of the status quo than heroic saints. Emphasizing the memorization of facts rather than encouragement of frank and free discussion deadens instead of arousing curiosity and understanding. Worrying more about protecting the young from the influence of evil than about urging them on to try to abolish it produces tension and timidity. In traditional education, as a general rule, private virtues ("the most important thing is to save your own soul") have been stressed far more than social ones, negative virtues ("avoid the occasion of sin") more than positive ones, and passive virtues (patience, politeness, neatness, quietness, obedience), which make a teacher's life easier, have been emphasized at the expense of active virtues (creativity, originality, initiative, courage, independence, eagerness, curiosity, generosity, enthusiasm), which make a student's life richer. Instead of sanctity, this priority of values produces repression and depression.

Methods of discipline, as well as the curriculum, have too often been unconsciously un-Christian. "Love is the whole law" and "love and do what thou wilt" are certainly not typical school slogans. Far too many petty, arbitrary rules have been laid down and rigidly enforced. When external conformity is considered more important than sincerity and spontaneity, one produces more hypocrites than heroes. When blind obedience to the voice of authority is demanded instead of alertness to the voice of conscience, one produces the kind of people who might obey a Hitler (perhaps we should actually be grateful to Hitler as an educator: thanks to him, in spite of us, many of our children have learned that there are times when *dis*obedience to authority is more virtuous than obedience).

The average parent has been as guilty of inculcating wrong values as the average teacher. The rod and the dunce cap have not been standard school equipment for many years, in this country at least (though subtler and almost as cruel forms of severity and ridicule do still exist in too many schools), but the majority of parents still rely heavily on spanking, thus making liars of themselves when they say such things as "Pick on someone your own size" and "Might doesn't make right." When we regularly use corporal punishment to enforce our will, what does it matter what we say about the power of love? We implant, deep down inside, the lasting conviction that might does make right and that physical force always has the last word in human relationships. People in authority who are unkind or petty or inconsistent teach unkindness and pettiness and inconsistency, no matter what they intend to teach. Children so treated become either wildly rebellious or cravenly dependent.

Many Catholics used to make fun of educational reformers whose ambition was to educate "the whole child," and who therefore stressed the value of play and physical exercise as much as that of academic work, who preferred animated discussions and original projects to monotonous drill, who advocated "democracy in the classroom" in the hope of developing a strong sense of personal responsibility in their pupils instead of abject fear of authoritarian rules, who tried to replace punishment with understanding guidance, who broadened the curriculum to emphasize "education for life" instead of sticking exclusively to the three R's, and who substituted conferences with parents for cut-and-dried report cards. Now that many of these "radical" and "progressive" and humane ideas have been practiced long enough to demonstrate their value, they are taken for granted by almost everyone and it is hard even to remember why they were ever so firmly resisted.

Was it because these ideas were un-Christian? Quite the contrary. They grew out of the desire to show more justice and love towards children than one could show by the old-fashioned methods that had been designed primarily for the convenience of adults. But we used to listen only to ideas that came properly labeled with the good churchgoer's seal of approval. It was *who* said something, not *what* someone said, that influenced us. When John Locke, in the eighteenth century, said, "A child's mind is not a pot to be filled but a fire to be kindled" all would-be teachers of saints would have agreed if they had listened, but he wasn't a Catholic so Catholics didn't listen. Fortunately, this kind of spiritual paranoia has been exorcised in our century.

The science of psychology, which was regarded with suspicion and hostility by Catholic educators, is now recognized as "the science of compassion" and a very useful handmaiden of morality. Its attempt to understand why people do what they do rather than to condemn and punish them whenever they do wrong may seem at first glance like moral indifference, but is it? No more than the study of anatomy or physics is. Psychologists have not yet been able to teach us (any more than moralists have) how to prevent evildoing, but they are on the right track, unless Christ didn't really mean it when he said people should help each other instead of judging each other. Morality tells us *what* we should do; psychology may eventually find out *how* we can do it.

Today, at last, education everywhere is wide open to new

approaches. Experimentation is the order of the day. We will continue, no doubt, to make mistakes — but at least they will not be the same mistakes we have made over and over again in the past. Education for brotherhood on a global scale is now a real possibility.

Social studies are replacing and expanding old concepts about history and geography. In the real world, ideas and facts are not tidily set apart in separate categories. Why teach history? Not in order to stuff heads with lots of ancient and irrelevant dates and names, but in order to develop appreciation of man's many achievements and possibilities, to learn the important lessons that our past can teach us, and to make use of these today and tomorrow. Why must geography be studied? Not primarily in order to memorize long lists of rivers and cities, but to learn how people, our brothers, live under different and difficult circumstances, and to know and understand and respect and aid them.

For education to sink in, and be worth learning, it must reach the sphere of action. One is not educated in order to amuse oneself in a sort of mental masturbation; one is educated in order to help the world. Riches are meant to be shared; if our education only enriches us it is wasted and incomplete, aborted. So children must be given frequent opportunities and vigorous encouragement to apply what they learn. School, like church, is a place where one should become inspired to go forth: *ite missa est*.

Education for peace must not be negative. Peace is not the mere absence of war any more than happiness is merely absence of anguish. A gardener has to do more than hate weeds; he has to work hard planting flowers. Teachers and parents have to do more than be against sin and error; they must plant and cultivate strong love of truth and beauty and goodness. Music and art and other peaceful pursuits demonstrate the glory of human beings' diversity. There is no one "right" or "wrong" way to paint; so when children are encouraged to produce their own unique creations, and to appreciate those of other people as well, they develop (without sermons) awareness of their own potentialities and those of other people too.

Education is not confined to the classroom, either. Children learn all day long every day. Bored, unguided children spend many hours fighting or pretend-fighting. Many little boys can think of nothing more entertaining than to play soldiers or cops and robbers or to watch grown-up actors playing the same thing on a TV screen. (People insist that gun-play is a harmless and healthy form of amusement that does not inculcate a love of violence, but if adult examples and juvenile activities do not influence growing children, then why do we not encourage little girls to shoot and beat their dolls instead of taking motherly care of them?) Culturally well-nourished children are too busy to concentrate on pointless fighting.

Schools and parents should launch youngsters on ambitious cooperative projects, teach them a large variety of games and crafts, skills involving all the senses (including the sense of humor) and the arts (including pleasant conversation) and ingenious ways of helping people — and such things should be taught with enthusiasm and joy. We should take our children to museums and theaters and concerts and sports events and faraway places often enough so that such occupations become enjoyable habits, not rare duties. When people know how to play hard *and* to work hard *and* enjoy both, they will not, out of sheer purposelessness, crave destructive "kicks" and "thrills."

We absorb the culture in our own environment without conscious effort, like our native language, whereas a conscious and conscientious effort has to be made by parents and teachers to make children aware of and appreciative of *other* cultures. A Catholic group in Brooklyn recently showed one imaginative way to do this. It was the only group in the entire United States to celebrate "Universal Children's Day" which the UN, eleven years ago, designated as an annual occasion on which to honor children and draw attention to their needs. Although this day is celebrated in over thirty countries, it had been ignored in the USA until the Catholic Guardian Society, an affiliate of Brooklyn Catholic Charities, decided to hold a party for the benefit of UNICEF. At this party seventy-five foster children toured eleven "foreign pavilions" to "meet" the children of other nations. On display were toys, games, records, pictures, schoolbooks, foods, and other articles representing children's lives in eleven foreign countries, and one child in each pavilion was dressed in the costume of the country.

It would be a good sign if this pleasant activity spread each year to more and more schools and parishes, linking children in an annual expression of worldwide friendship. It could happen. The annual "Trick or Treat for UNICEF" campaign, in which more than 10,000,000 American and Canadian children take part — raising several million dollars every year to buy medicine, vitamins, milk, food, and schoolbooks for children who would otherwise lack them — was started a few years ago on the private initiative of a small Sunday School class in Pennsylvania. The children thought up the idea and mailed the money they collected ($17) to UNICEF. Most grown-ups would have thought you could not help the international situation with a mere $17. Children encouraged to act upon generous impulses know better, like the boy who gave up the little he had and then witnessed the miracle of the loaves and fishes.

It is depressing, however, to learn that only one percent of the Catholic schools and parishes in the US join with the other children of their communities in the "Trick or Treat" campaign. While atheistic, agnostic, Protestant, and Jewish children are having fun setting a remarkable example of cooperative generosity and seeing movies and reading booklets about the lives of children all around the world, learning that individuals when they work together have the power to accomplish great and lasting good that changes the world for the better, most Catholic children are honoring the vigil of All Saints Day by demanding for themselves more candy than they can possibly eat without a stomach ache and more money than they can possibly spend except on things they do not need.

Catholic children contribute regularly to the missions, of course, but the emphasis in these collections is not usually very educational. Too much stress is put on money, which teaches materialism. Competitiveness among the children about the amounts collected is encouraged, which teaches them to show off and boast and be jealous. Helping "pagan" babies often merely means getting them baptized with American or European names, which teaches the contributors to feel sure they belong to a superior culture. And concentrating exclusively on Catholic projects teaches spiritual isolationism. When we only help "our" missions we cannot learn the value of joining with others in doing good. When our only relationship to the poor is to send them money, we do not learn to love the poor. What we really learn is to love ourselves for being so generous.

It is wonderful to help missionary activities, certainly, if it isn't to the exclusion of helping other useful and important causes sponsored by other people. When money is raised for missionaries or for anyone else, however, how the money is raised is almost as important as what it is raised for. Why are bingo, roulette, raffles, and begging the main methods used? There are so many more meaningful, creative ways to raise money: by putting on puppet shows, educational films, concerts, dance recitals; by having art and photography essay contests, debates on current events, bazaars where handmade crafts and toys are exhibited and sold, parties for which children plan and make their own attractive decorations.

Said Pope Paul:

> Brotherly cooperation among people is the finest aspect of the United Nations, its most truly human aspect, the ideal mankind dreams of on its pilgrimage through time, the world's greatest hope . . . the reflection of the loving and transcendent design of God for the progress of the human family on earth—a reflection in which we see the heavenly message of the Gospel made earthly.

Like anything else, brotherly cooperation can only be learned through practice.

Of the UN delegates Pope Paul asked:

> Will the world ever succeed in changing that selfish and bellicose mentality which, up to now, has been interwoven

with so much of its history? It is hard to forsee. But it is easy to affirm that it is toward that new history, as promised by God to men of goodwill, that we must resolutely march.

If America survives its present moral and military crisis, will we sit back with a sigh of relief and give up our efforts to do all we can to promote lasting peace and universal brotherhood, on the grounds that the problem is no longer urgent? After every war in the past, chastened people have resolved that it would never happen again. Can we teach our children to learn from our mistakes so that they will not have to repeat them? We can if we want to enough and if we ourselves recognize and admit them.

In *Pacem in Terris,* Pope John said the same moral law that binds individuals binds nations. Do we believe this? People who would never *personally* injure a child face the fact that their country injures hundreds and thousands of children, without feeling deep indignation or shame, because "all's fair in love and war." Unfortunately, in practice, isn't it more apt to work the other way around? National morals influence personal morals. The mass violence a country's soldiers participate in on foreign soil gradually poisons their native soil. Poorly educated, confused, frustrated and unbalanced people see their country's esteemed policymakers justifying undeclared war and the bombing of villages. Its system of justice puts believers in nonviolence in jail. Its budget-makers allocate billions of dollars for guns but balk at spending far less money on schools or slum clearance or aid to developing nations. Its legislators consider it more vital to preserve the "right" to buy guns than to make shopping difficult for assassins. The result is tragically logical: newspaper headlines shriek, in ever accelerating crescendos, about thefts, assaults, murders, kidnappings, divorces, riots, battles, threats and acts of brutal and irrational violence. City streets and parks are no longer safe places to walk. All over our "peace-loving" land hoodlums and bullies and emotional people with real and/or imagined grievances feel justified in robbing and killing. If their country has the right and even "duty" to enforce its views by means of guns, they cannot see why individuals do not.

All the achievements of civilization, so slowly built up through centuries of effort, are threatened by the methods with which we have chosen to "protect" civilization. But there are signs of hope, too, even now. Arnold Toynbee, in one of his increasingly rare optimistic moments, said our century may go down in history not for its dreadful wars but as the first one in which men realized that the benefits of civilization must extend to *all* mankind. Universal brotherhood, once a high but only vaguely understood ideal, has now become a real necessity and a practical possibility for the first time. Modern science is giving us unprecedented power to destroy each other *and* to help each other, through new medical, psychological, educational and sociological techniques; it is giving us great, frightening dangers *and* at the same time, providentially, stronger incentives and greater opportunities to do good.

Alongside the tragic war in Vietnam, what the United Nations calls "The Good War" is being vigorously fought on many fronts. In every country there are people living dedicated lives that are as adventurous and thrilling as those of any soldier of fortune. They travel around the globe to strange and exotic places, slaying dragons (germs and superstitions) and fighting devils (ignorance, poverty, greed, apathy, corruption) as heroically as knights in ancient legends ever did. When one has an opportunity to meet such people one realizes how beautiful and exciting life (and peace) can be. When will our newspaper writers and television producers give such people equal time with gangsters and military soldiers? When will peacemakers replace gun-toters as our folk heroes?

Recently the Freedom-from-Hunger Campaign sponsored by FAO held an international meeting of young people from every continent, the climax of a series of student seminars in many countries. The participants drew up a *Young World Manifesto* in which they declared: "Our generation has power and knowledge that no previous generation has ever had. With these we must create a world in which the human spirit is set free from hunger and want, forever."

More than half the people in the world today are under 25 years old. Let us hope they have the energy, intelligence, generosity and skill to succeed where their parents have failed. And let us hope that we ourselves can find the courage and wisdom to guide them or at least to accompany them part of the way in their efforts to achieve a better world than the one they have inherited. At the very least, let us not continue to throw roadblocks — due to prejudice, timidity, cynicism, and more epidemics of mass murder — on the path along which they and their brothers will walk together into the future.

6. The Churches and Conscription

Philip J. Scharper

NEVER PERHAPS IN THE LONG LEGAL HISTORY OF THE United States had the wide net of the Justice Department landed two such big fish of quite different species: Cassius Clay, charged with draft evasion despite his claim to be a Black Muslim minister, and Dr. Benjamin Spock, to whose varying counsels millions of Americans have been exposed over four generations through successive editions of his do-it-yourself pediatrics. Dr. Spock's offense was that he had encouraged young men of draft age to evade the national laws governing universal military conscription.

The net, flung wider than ever in the year 1967, had, of course, also brought in a number of small and intermediate size fish, many of them of quite surprising species. Reverend Philip Berrigan was arrested, together with a minister and two laymen, and later convicted, for pouring blood on the draft records maintained by the Federal government in Baltimore. Another Catholic priest, serving in the student ministry at Cornell University, lost his preferential status in the draft because he had publicly counselled college students to burn or turn in their draft cards.

Perhaps no one of these incidents — or the dozens of others which have been widely reported in the press — is significant in itself. What is significant is that the Clays and the Berrigans, the Spocks and the Coffins have served as voices for many thousands of Americans who, whatever might be their differences in race, religion, or educational background, have found themselves increasingly united by their questioning of and active opposition to the drafting of American males for military service.

The strident chorus of "Hell no, we won't go!" has not replaced the singing of Alma Mater at college commencements, nor the rhythmic exhortations to "Hold that line!" addressed to varsity football teams on autumn afternoons in crowded stadia. But the chorus is growing stronger in number and volume and, once more, the fact that it is being chanted by Ivy League students as well as by those in the Negro colleges of the deep South gives the rising chorus its particular significance.

Similarly, such religious figures as Father Berrigan and Dr. William Sloane Coffin, Jr., are not lonely voices shouting against the wind. Well over a thousand seminarians have asked that their exemption under law, the IV-D classification for theological students and clergymen, be abrogated and that they be made subject to the same drafting procedures and policies as are the remainder of the population. The influential journal *Christianity and Crisis* (April 17, 1967) urged in a lead editorial that the IV-D classification be completely abolished, since such exemption seemed "bizarre and unfair, especially at a time when the churches are declaiming about the ministry of the laity and the shared priesthood of the entire people of God."

In the past, both in the United States and other Western countries, religious groups have not established a notable record for their opposition to the written laws and announced military programs and procedures of their respective nations. Indeed, the Christian churches have been almost ritualistic in the support of their countries' policies — particularly in time of war, when the hymn "Onward Christian Soldiers" was frequently given a completely secularistic understanding by the churches as they sent their sons off to battle with benedictions and huzzahs. Why, then, have individual religious spokesmen and entire church groups begun to act in a somewhat prophetic fashion in the United States within the last few years? In some instances they have not sent forth their military-age adherents to combat, but have offered their churches as sanctuaries for those who would refuse military conscription and would seek protection from the usual legal consequences of fine and/or imprisonment.

There are, of course, many reasons. History seldom gives us the luxury of a single cause that will explain a sudden reversal of human behavior such as we have been witnessing in the growing religious resistance to the draft in the United States. Here, however, we shall attempt to deal with only a few of the many reasons, selecting for our attention those that seem to have the most observable resonance.

(1) *Unpopularity of the Vietnam War.* Although at no time in its history has the draft in the United States been so opposed, defied, evaded, and scrutinized as it is today, most of those who have commented, either in question or support of the draft, have overlooked its correlation with the war in Vietnam.

Obviously, the American action in Vietnam is unpopular, i.e., tolerated rather than supported, by the majority of Americans, even by those Americans who have not opposed the war. The fact that over half a million Americans are still in Vietnam has made a growing number of Americans restive, and has increased the number of citizens who are attempting to bring an end to our Vietnam involvement through other than military means. Among men of draft age, the war itself, with its clouded objectives and the Administration's smoke-screen handling of facts concerning it, has induced a mood of resistance and cynicism, with a corresponding decline in the acceptance of the legitimacy of the draft in a democracy. The Second World War, for example, saw comparatively little resistance to the draft other than by those who were, in conscience, opposed to any and all wars.

The fact that the Vietnam war, unlike the other major wars involving America in this century, has been seen to be not only dirty and expensive in its execution, but also inconclusive in its objectives and dubious in its results, has served to bring under close scrutiny the very draft process which is necessary to supply the number of American troops seemingly necessary to fight an undeclared war to its uncertain conclusions.

(2) *The Inequalities of the Draft.* A legislative committee composed of Plato, Thomas Jefferson, Mahatma Gandhi, and Jesus of Nazareth could not, obviously, draft legislation for compulsory military service that would remove from its operation every conceivable inadequacy and inequality. Even recognizing the inevitable shortcomings of the wisest and most humane legislation in this area, one must point out that the present draft legislation and implementation in the United States is weak with rust, creaks with age, and proliferates inequalities that reach into almost every area of American life.

Local draft boards, guided by obscure and often contradictory criteria, decide the fate of millions. There is astonishing variation from state to state in the classification of men who are deferred from military service. Thus in one state married men are subject to the draft; in other states they are not. Peace Corps volunteers are drafted in Kansas, but deferred in New York. Illinois gives special consideration to those training to become morticians, but Alabama does not.

The inequalities and lack of democratic representation are seen more clearly when it is realized that draft board members throughout the nation are all male, mostly veterans, white-collar workers, and are virtually all white. Only 1.3 percent of draft board members are Negroes, although the number of Negroes drafted is far higher in proportion than is the number of whites of military age. Twenty-two percent of draft board members are over seventy years of age, and the average age is fifty-eight. Although it was the intention of Congress, in its initial draft legislation, that selective service be controlled by civilians, its top officials are heavily military in orientation and training.

It is possible to put some of these inequities in rather sharp focus. Forty percent of the population of New Orleans is Negro and 60 percent of the casualties in Vietnam from New Orleans are Negro. Yet no Negro has ever served on a draft board in that city.

The inequities resulting from educational deferments can be seen in the fact that less than 6 percent of all draftees are college graduates — a fact which led President Brewster of Yale to state that a policy of selecting only those "who cannot hide in the endless catacombs of formal education" is a mockery.

(3) *The Question of Conscience.* There have, of course, been pacifists who objected to service in both World Wars and the Korean War — the wars covered by our present method of selective service. Those who object to participation in any war, on grounds that such participation would violate their conscience, are specially exempted from military service by the draft legislation that offers the status of conscientious objector to those who are "conscientiously opposed to participation in war in any form."

The question assuming ever greater importance today, however, centers not on the exemption from military service of the complete pacifist, but exemption for the *selective* pacifist, the individual who is not opposed to "war in any form," but is opposed only to a specific war, notably the war in Vietnam. It is this question to which the churches have been addressing themselves with a strength and solidity notably missing from the reaction of church bodies to American participation in either the Korean War or the Second World War.

Thus, for example, the Second Vatican Council in its *Constitution on the Church in the Modern World* indicated its defense of the right to conscientious objection, and the pastoral statement of the U.S. Bishops on Peace and Vietnam said, "No one is free to evade his personal responsibility by leaving it entirely to others to make moral judgements."

It is particularly interesting to note, in this connection, that the present Selective Service system seems, in the opinion of many, to be particularly unfair to Roman Catholics. Catholics who are true to the teaching of the Church must in conscience oppose participation in wars that do not meet the traditional Catholic teaching on the conditions of the just war. If, in the opinion of a given Roman Catholic, the Vietnam war does not fulfill the conditions of being just and is therefore immoral, he cannot qualify as a conscientious objector because he cannot show that his church is opposed to "war in any form."

This "discrimination" against Catholics was the subject of a memorandum sent to the National Conference of Catholic Bishops in April 1967 by the American Pax Association, a group of "Catholics and others who seek to promote peace and to encourage the practical application of Christian principles to the question of war." In its memorandum, Pax asked the bishops to appoint a special committee to prepare a statement on military conscription, since the Selective Service system was, at that time, under review before it was to be legally renewed on July 1, 1967. But Congress went about the task of revising the Selective Service legislation untroubled by any communiques from the U.S. Conference of Catholic Bishops.

The principle of selective conscientious objection was considered by the President's National Advisory Commission on Selective Service but was, in the end, overwhelmingly rejected. As a consequence, the revision of the Selective Service Act, effective July 1, 1967, limited the status of conscientious objector for all practical purposes to members of the "peace churches" such as Quakers and the Mennonites.

In October of 1967 the Catholic Association for International Peace held its fortieth annual conference; the theme of the discussion was Selective Conscientious Objection. The fact, however, that the selective conscientious objector had already been discriminated against in legislation passed three months prior to the conference gave the discussions of the CAIP a rather academic ring. The question raised several years before by the late John Courtney Murray still remained the question:

> Strictly on the grounds of moral argument, the right conscientiously to object to participation in a particular war is incontestable . . . the practical question before all of us is how to get the moral validity of this right understood, and how to get the right itself legally recognized and declared in statutory law.

The implementation of Father Murray's "practical question" must presumably await the next revision of the Selective Service Act or be settled in the streets. The next revision of the Selective Service Act will be in 1971; the failure of Congress in 1967 to examine anew the position of the selective conscientious objector offers such a person the unworthy options of: (i) giving false statements to his selective service board, (ii) fleeing the country, as thousands have already done, or (iii) spending up to five years in prison. A nation that continually reminds itself of its roots in both the democratic and Judeo-Christian traditions might be expected to show in its laws a greater respect for the integrity of the individual conscience.

Such was the contention of the Committee of Clergy and Laymen Concerned about Vietnam, which issued in September 1967 one of the strongest statements on the draft yet to appear from any religiously oriented group.

> We pledge ourselves to a national program offering information, advice, encouragement and protection to young men who cannot in conscience participate in the military forces or in a particular operation of the same. We pledge ourselves to those who, already in the military forces, refuse to obey orders directing them to commit acts which they believe to be criminal and in violation of conscience. We pledge ourselves to those who, already in the military forces, feel compelled by conscience to separate themselves from the military. If such person can find no remedy in existing laws, we will accept them as refugees from injustice. We offer churches and synagogues as places of refuge, in accord with the ancient tradition of religious sanctuary (Deuteronomy 19, Joshua 20).

What are the alternatives to the draft?

(1) *The Lottery.* In its consideration of the Selective Service Act the President's National Advisory Commission, chaired by Burke Marshall, made a recommendation that drew considerable public discussion but was not adopted by Congress. The Marshall Commission had suggested that the basis for drawing men into military service should be a system of random selection — in effect, a lottery. The reasons for the suggestion of a lottery were, principally, these: so many young men turn eighteen every year (two million by 1970) that student and occupational deferments are no longer needed to insure necessary supplies of manpower in so-called essential occupations. The armed forces require only a small minority of the men available.

If the men needed by the military were selected at random, through a Federal lottery, only a fraction of the young would be touched, and the political-moral problems of inequities would be eased since draftees would be drawn, with impartial arbitrariness, from all races, areas and economic levels. The possible objection about inserting a large element of uncertainty into the lives of the young men in American society would also be eliminated by drafting first the younger men who are, in any case, considered more malleable by the military.

In the long run, however, it seems unlikely that the lottery system recommended by the Marshall Commission will fare any better in 1971 than it did in 1967. One who reads American history cannot close the book without feeling that the American people, for whatever mixed reasons, will not tolerate a Selective Service system in which a fraction of the young people make sacrifices — including the supreme sacrifice — because they have lost a game of roulette. Las Vegas has not yet become a symbol for the workings of democratic society at war.

(2) *Alternative Services.* In the increasingly heated discussion of the draft, attention has been paid to the possibilities of alternative service, whereby an individual who could not in conscience bear arms or assist those who carried the military objectives of the nation might nonetheless serve his country and mankind by servicing economic and social needs.

At its annual meeting in February 1968 the American Pax Association passed a resolution asking the American Catholic bishops to provide

> a channel so that young Catholics "who have chosen in conscience the works of mercy over the works of war may participate in overseas programs in underdeveloped areas." The statement pointed out that the other church-related aid agencies make good use of conscientious objectors in their overseas programs, while Catholic Relief Services, the only Catholic agency recognized by Selective Service for alternative service never makes use of conscientious objectors. The group asked that the bishops correct this in view of the sentiments expressed in "The Church in the Modern World" and "The

Development of Peoples" both of which praise the witness of nonviolence as long as the person is willing to serve the human community in ways other than military.

Indeed, the Marshall Commission itself had suggested vast programs of "national service," in which young people would be "expected" to serve as police trainees, teachers, job or peace corpsmen, etc. if they were not drafted under the Commission's suggested lottery.

Two immediate reactions leap to mind from the Marshall suggestion. One, it would mean an acceleration of the control already exercised by the government over individual destinies. Those not picked up for military service in the lottery system would be "expected" to perform national service — not necessarily according to the young citizen's interest or abilities, but by the computerized decision of a central manpower commission. To speak of American youth as a "national resource," as the Marshall Commission does, is to speak with the voice of Jacob but to push the levels of dictatorial control over human lives with the hairy hands of Esau.

The second reaction to the Marshall suggestion (which was not, of course, adopted by Congress in any case) is to recall, with a shudder, that some draft boards had inducted men who were serving in either Vista or Peace Corps programs, without effective protest from the national directors of these federally sponsored and funded programs. The national mood, obviously, is to beat the plowshares into swords.

(3) *A Volunteer Army.* An interesting lateral development of the draft debate has been the raising of a question unasked for half a century in the United States: if a large standing army is, seemingly, a necessary instrument of our national policies, should that army not be composed of volunteers, rather than of draftees?

Indeed, Senator Barry Goldwater in the election campaign of 1964 had suggested that a volunteer army was feasible. Senator Goldwater's suggestion certainly did not stir national discussion, but it aroused interest sufficient to prompt President

Johnson to order a Defense Department study of the possibility.

Never fully published, the resulting study urged the continuance of the draft system, principally because of the staggering sums needed to hire an army of sufficient size to meet America's growing military-manpower needs.

Our concern here is not with the financial argument, but rather with the human values at stake in the draft versus volunteer discussion. It is, however, worth noting the point made by Bruce K. Chapman (*The Wrong Man in Uniform,* Trident, 1967). The pay of an army private, he points out, is little more than that of a Rumanian peasant on a collective farm. Give men freedom to choose, Chapman continues, pay them a decent wage — in short, apply the techniques of effective business management — and the nation could produce an efficient, stable military "work force" at a socially acceptable and fiscally tolerable cost.

A quite different argument in support of a volunteer army was provided by the American Pax Association in its memorandum to the Catholic Bishops of April 3, 1967.

Recalling that student representatives of National Newman Federation, the University Christian Movement, the YMCA, the YWCA, and Pax Romana had called for an end to the draft, the Pax statement continued:

> The volunteer army plan does less violence to the Catholic concept of individual vocation than does the coercion inherent in any system of military conscription. Catholics of today have seemingly forgotten that the system of universal military training grew up completely outside the Catholic tradition and that it was repeatedly condemned by the churchmen of the day. The universal draft that we know today was a product of the French Revolution and of the Prussian State. It was quite clear when the French state became a "nation in arms" through universal recruitment that this system was in conflict with the concept of freedom of vocation so central to Catholic life.

Again, there was no response from the bishops, nor any subsequent indication that the volunteer army as a "Christian" alternative to the draft would be the subject of their further inquiry. In the judgment of the present writer, a remarkable opportunity was thus lost to exert spiritual leadership in a time of doubt and crisis for the consciences of thousands under their charge.

In all likelihood, the storm of debate and protest now swirling around the draft will grow stronger and more violent, but will never become strong enough really to change the situation. The nation seems to accept the draft with a fatalism akin to that with which one accepts floods and fires.

This fatalistic acceptance of the draft is closely linked, of course, to the larger fact that Americans seemingly have come to accept with but little reflection and no questioning: The United States has become a massive war-machine, and cultural and social concerns are increasingly crushed beneath the juggernaut.

In attempting to police the world through military power rather than through diplomacy or with allies, we have embarked upon a course more dangerous and costly than has any empire of the past.

Since World War II, we have spent over $900 billion on military needs, less than 1/10 that amount for health, education, welfare, housing, and community development. Although exact figures are hard to come by, our expenditure in Vietnam has averaged perhaps $3 billion per month; the Interior Department is calling for $2 billion per year as the necessary minimum for new sewers and treatment plants to make our water safe — but this money may not be forthcoming. Our reckless expenditure of money is, of course, but a symbol of our reckless expenditure of men: we may be mortgaging our future by the expenditure of both.

The issue of the draft, then, is larger than the question of how we raise an army. It is the issue, rather, of whether, as a nation, we will once more give priority to personal freedom and the building of a just society, or whether we will pour out our treasures of men and money in support of a policy requiring military intervention on a global scale. This is the issue pressed like a knife edge against the American conscience.

7. Draft Board Theology

MICHAEL NOVAK

THE ALTERNATIVES FACING MOST YOUNG MEN OF draft age who oppose the war in Vietnam are cruel: five years in jail or emigration from the United States. Most cannot answer honestly the theologically outmoded and discriminatory form for conscientious objection supplied by the Selective Service system. A Christian theologian would not be able to assent to the form as it is now written; the form, moreover, seems to put local draft boards in the position of playing inquisitor — sending boys who answer falteringly to war, jail, or exile. Could the men who made up the questions on SSS Form No. 150 pass an examination in theology? Not in this century.

The first question the form asks is: "Do you believe in a Supreme Being?" One must answer "Yes" or "No." Any young man who has read Paul Tillich knows that this stark choice poses an impossible dilemma. To call God "a" Being, even a "Supreme" Being, is to make him into an object among other objects, and hence to fall into idolatry. In the ordinary sense of "being," God cannot be called a being. Most young men in the colleges find it impossible to believe in a God who is "a being," even a Supreme Being (somewhere out there). A theologically untrained older generation may think of God as "Supreme Being," but many in the younger generation emphatically do not.

Next the candidates are told: "Describe the nature of your belief which is the basis of your claim . . . and state whether or not your belief in a Supreme Being involves duties which are superior to those arising from any human relation." Many young men know of no duties except those that arise from human relations. If they use the word "God" at all, it is in connection with certain experiences they have in and only in human relations. In this they agree with the most distinguished Catholic theologian of the older generation, Karl Rahner, who has recently argued in *Theological Investigations VI* that love of God is identical with love of man.

Again, the young do not think in terms of "duty." They think in terms of "responsibility," in which the key idea is "response" — respectful response to the reality of other persons. Their notion of God derives from experiences of human relations. "How can you love God whom you do not see, if you do not love your neighbor whom you do see?" (I John 4). They find something in human relations that makes human relations superior to any other part of life. They would be willing to leave mother, father, wife, sister, brother, in the name of conscience — but they think of conscience itself as a form of interpersonal relations. How can one have any human relation at all unless one keeps personal integrity? Such integrity makes mutual love possible. Such integrity, moreover, is dependent on mutual love and impossible without it. There is no duty "superior to" the responsibilities of human relations so conceived. God is present in human relations and is not known in any other way.

Perhaps the trouble arises because the folk religion of the Selective Service apparently distinguishes "duties towards God" from "duties towards family" and "duties towards country" and, reluctantly, gives priority to the first. The more acute theology of the young holds that God (if one must use that much cheapened name) is present through the light of personal conscience in human relations. God is not thought of as separate and "above" family and nation. Family and nation apart from the light of personal conscience are salt without savor, good for nothing but to be trampled on by men. The young do not adore family or nation or any other human relation.

They place conscience above family and nation. But this conscience develops in and through human relations. It is not "superior to" them but their very heart and core. "I looked for you everywhere, my God," St. Augustine wrote, "but when I found you, you were within me."

Thirdly, the candidate is asked to explain, "How, when and from whom and from what sources you received the training and acquired the belief which is the basis of your claim?" The answer for many candidates would entail citing sources the draft board members may not recognize or, recognizing, may fear: Herman Hesse, Albert Camus, Jean-Paul Sartre, Dostoevsky, Tillich, Bonhoeffer, the Nuremberg trials. The source is unlikely to be a church, a minister, priest, or nun; it is unlikely to be parents. Almost certainly the source will be books, most often by existentialist philosophers or theologians. Who else writes so centrally on the importance of conscience? The other common sources will be friends who led one to the books.

Consequently, question four, "Give the name and present address of the individual upon whom you rely most for religious guidance," is pretty silly. The expected answer seems to assume that Americans still live in small towns where they have known the local minister since they were knee-high, and he stands ready to testify to one's goodness, seriousness, and piety. In fact, most college students know no adult at all to whom they go for guidance — no one minister, and almost certainly not even one professor. The mobility and impersonality of contemporary life makes the word "guidance" quaint. Students are on their own. They make do with friends, conversations, public lectures, and books. They are often either fiercely conformist or fiercely independent.

Finally, asked to answer, "Under what circumstances, if any, do you believe in the use of force?", most students would have to say that they would probably approve of the attempt by Dietrich Bonhoeffer and others to assassinate Hitler. They would use force to halt a drunken driver — possibly even if he were the captain of their own ship of state. But they wish to reserve the judgment over "circumstances" to themselves.

They will not merely obey orders, not from army commanders, not even from the chief of state. The Nuremberg declaration does not allow them to surrender such judgment into anyone else's hands.

In short, the conscience of many young men and also of contemporary theology demands new standards for conscientious objection. Do we want all those who hate the violence of the brutal, mistaken war in Vietnam to go to jail or to leave our shores? Do we want the voice of conscience crushed and oppressed? Do we want an ever larger police state? The present draft law is intolerable. The form for conscientious objection is a theological disgrace.

Recently, I have seen too many splendid young men mentally and emotionally broken by the threefold choice between (1) killing other human beings in an unnecessary and evil war, (2) going to jail for five years, or (3) leaving their native land. They cannot bear this strain alone. I know that it is a felony punishable by the same penalties they face — up to five years in jail or a fine up to $10,000 — to aid, abet, or encourage men to resist the draft. In order to share the burden of an unjust and stupid draft law, I would like to join those who aid, abet, and encourage young men to resist the draft. Many must resist, until the conscience of a sleeping and silly nation is awakened. There are worse things than jail — living in a nation, for example, that cares so little about justice and peace. To be sure, the words "justice" and "peace" are ever on the lips of politicians, ministers of God, and the slumbering people in whose name so many deaths are being inflicted daily. But the United States cherishes the myth of anti-Communism more than it cherishes justice and peace. We have duped ourselves into being warriors and crusaders. We are paying for our blindness with the mangled bodies of young men. Our blindness is not worth that price: not of a single living human being, surely not of the young men with whom many of us daily live.

American Catholics and Vietnam

8. Catholicism, Power, and Vietnamese Suffering

JAMES W. DOUGLASS

AMERICANS LIVE UNDER A CURSE. IT IS THE CURSE OF Jesus: "Depart from me, you cursed Americans, into the eternal fire prepared for the devil and his angels; for I was a hungry North Vietnamese and you gave me no food, I was a thirsty Viet Cong and you gave me no drink, I was a napalmed child and you did not welcome me. . . . In fact, it is you who made me, the Vietnamese Christ, hungry and thirsty, an outlaw hiding out in my own forests, and it is you who maintain my suffering by bombing my people and villages and razing my land" (Matthew 25, contemporary reading).

If the Christ of American Catholicism does not usually speak in this manner, it is because he is more American than Catholic, and more anti-Communist than American. The Christ of the Gospels does not have this problem. He speaks for all men and stands willingly with them when they suffer and die. "As you did it not to one of the least of these, you did it not to me." The Christ of the Gospels is more the Christ of the National Liberation Front than he is the Christ of American Catholics. For the NLF, which is no community of saints, at least stands willingly in the midst of the suffering, where Christ has always said he stood, while American Catholics for the most part stand with the oppressors and bless their holy war. This is not to deny American Catholics their good faith and conscience. It is simply to say that with respect to Vietnam theirs is a faith in someone other than Jesus Christ.

The "Samaritan" whom Jesus sets forth as a symbol of his own response to suffering sounded in contemporary Jewish ears like "Chinese Communist" does in ours. The mortal enemy in Jesus' terms is neither Samaria nor China, but our own lack of compassion. The question then is: How has American Catholicism contributed to this country's lack of compassion for Vietnam? And because the absence of love is a vacuum inevitably filled by brute power: What is the relation between American power and Vietnamese suffering?

One begins with the fact of American Catholic support of the President's war. The polls tell us that the percentage of U.S. Catholics in favor of the war and even of intensifying it is higher than that of either Protestants or Jews. As to why this is so, various reasons suggest themselves: authoritarianism in the Church that has traditionally made it easier to polarize Catholic opinion into cold-war axioms; the anti-Communist legacy of the papacy before John; the distance, until fairly recently, between Catholic eyes and ears and scriptural sources of belief, which would reveal to them (but have only begun to do so) a Christ who judges rather than reflects political and cultural dogmas.

Perhaps more basic than any of these elements that contribute to war, and underlying them all, has been the popular theology of politics of American Catholicism, beginning with the externalization of all evil in "them" — Russians, Chinese, Viet Cong and North Vietnamese, Communist revolutionaries, and down the street, Black Power leaders. The enemy is that other; his evil is absolute; my salvation is his death or defeat. God is not simply on my side; he is the servant of my fear, the justifier of my weapons and belligerence, who blesses in battle us who are usually equipped with overwhelmingly superior firepower.

It is true that Catholics hold this polarized theology of fear in common with most other Americans. Americans from Shirley Temple to Dean Rusk are all inclined toward a highly polarized vision of good and evil, whether in terms of the Old West or of national power realities. But however convinced many

Americans may be of the enemy's particular evil, most of them have only a vague notion of evil itself. The enemy is evil, but evil itself is a relative factor and has only a vague foundation in reality. For these Americans, evil is subject to the counter-acting growth and progress of whatever it is that sustains American optimism — technological advance more than any-thing else.

For the American Catholic, however, evil is not only a political fact in the enemy but a dogmatic certitude of faith. Sin is a permanent fact in the world. Moreover, popular dis-tortions of Satan and original sin have created in the American Catholic a sense of evil as an absolute. Satan, it would seem in this perspective, can incarnate himself in history more easily than can God. God has become incarnate only in Christ. Satan has been fully manifest in Hitler, Stalin, Communists everywhere, and a host of odd revolutionaries from Malcolm X to Rap Brown. A belief in absolute evil, externalized and multiplied, joined with a static belief in the incarnation of Christ, becomes a summons to absolute power.

The American Catholic may identify Christ messianically with the destiny of America, as Father Daniel Lyons does, but he will do so in such a way that Christ's power is indistinguishable from the instruments of American nationalism. Father Lyons is very strong on weapons. God is thought to will our victory over Satan with the most terrible power we can bring to bear on him. After all, the Apocalypse seems to show God himself resorting to such power to vanquish Satan. God blesses our arsenal because of the absolute evil we perceive against us. Thus in the absence of a Christ whose power is distinguishable from modern weapons, and confronted by absolute evil, enor-mous technological power becomes our only defense against the red dragon. In such fashion is the popular theological frame-work for the battle constructed. Once we stand within it, all the evident evils of our own actions can be minimized in contrast to the absolute evil posed against us, and can be justified as "unintended."

Vietnamese suffering cannot be attributed directly to a vulgarized Catholic theology of absolute evil. Nevertheless, as an enveloping structure for the political faith of the largest religious group supporting the President's escalations, its influence is significant. This theology of absolute evil has also had significant influence upon American Catholic efforts to alleviate the suffering of the Vietnamese.

By now it is well known from reports in *The National Catholic Reporter* and *The New York Times* that Catholic Relief Services, the overseas relief agency of the Church in the United States, for more than a year distributed half of its food rations in Vietnam to the South Vietnamese militia. The step of directing this food supply each month to the South Vietnamese Government's local military forces and families was undertaken by CRS as a wage increase to the soldiers requested by U.S. General William Westmoreland. Only the remainder of the CRS food was thus available for refugees, orphans, and school children in South Vietnam, and nothing was given by CRS to North Vietnam. The action of the relief agency of the American Church stands in contrast to Caritas Internationalis, the Vatican-based relief body, which has sent medical supplies to North Vietnam.

Thus the corollary of overwhelming firepower to contend with absolute evil is an apparent powerlessness to undertake any action of a distinctively Christian character. As the bishop who is the executive director of CRS has said with regard to helping suffering civilians in North Vietnam, "It would be a holy and just thing to do. But it is simply impossible." Apparently it was almost as impossible to distribute aid effectively in South Vietnam except to and through the Saigon regime's militia. American Catholicism is helpless to help the Vietnamese because Satan controls Vietnam and Christ works through proper American channels. The "impossibility" of the task has not been granted by Pope Paul and Caritas or by other Christian service organizations working in Vietnam independently of the Saigon regime. The American Church has contributed an ideology of Christian impotence to justify the inaction of love and the steady enlargement of American power.

The larger relation between American power and Vietnamese suffering is the relation between Pilate and Christ. A fascinating aspect of the Gospels is their sympathetic characterization of Pilate. Pilate was deeply interested in Jesus. His dialogue with Jesus is a probing effort to uncover some excuse for acquittal. His offer of Barabbas to the chief priests and the crowd is another attempt to avoid executing Jesus, whom his wife had suffered over in a dream. Pilate was clearly "a man of good will," placed by circumstances in a difficult position. But Pilate was a politician, and politics, as we all know, is the art of the possible. It is obvious that it was politically impossible to avoid executing Jesus. Pilate did all he could to avoid the step and finally took the only course of action he could as governor. Being a man of good will, he washed his hands of the decision, then with reluctance "having scourged Jesus, he delivered him to be crucified."

Pilate, like many American leaders and citizens who are disturbed over Vietnam, was willing to try every alternative he could conceive of to avoid a murderous use of power. But as a man of power mindful of his other commitments he found it impossible not to sacrifice Jesus. Mankind's primary recollection of him is therefore not his agony over his decision but the simple fact that Jesus "suffered under Pontius Pilate." However reasonable it may have seemed in terms of the realities of power, murder remains murder. More important, Golgotha remains present. Pilate is the troubled American doing his duty high over the jungles and rice paddies and releasing his load of bombs. Pilate is several million concerned faces watching the daily slaughter on the TV screen, hesitant and helpless over their own lack of power to change the facts of power. Pilate washes his hands and prepares for dinner. Pilate is well intentioned but Pilate is irresponsible. Pilate is the chief murderer in history.

In the case of Vietnam, Pilate is not the American soldier, himself usually from the bottom of the society that sends him to war, and like the enemy, a victim. Pilate is the man who sends him there or who watches helplessly from the safety of affluence while the American soldier dies blindly and needlessly. Pilate is the impotent man of power — the man who writes these words, or who reads them, and does nothing else.

If "Catholicism" is anything more than a proper name, it is a recognition of the universal presence of Christ in man. The gospel defines the nature of this presence. Christ is present passively as man's suffering need. He is present actively as man's suffering response in love to that need. More profoundly, in an ontological perspective, Christ is that openness in man that signifies the union between Son and Father in love. But in the immediate drama of life, where openness is a wound, Christ is man's agonizing cry for life, and in turn, his brother's answer of life to that cry. Human need and human response converge in community. Life at the heart of the world confirms the gospel's insight that Christ is present in man as suffering love drawing him into community. The dogmatic definition of Christ as the man-God provides the background for his human significance in the world. Christ's central or existential meaning for man is suffering love, which redeems man from his violence to himself and to his brother and into the community of mutual human recognition.

With respect to American power and Vietnamese suffering, the living meaning of Catholicism is identification with the suffering need of the Vietnamese Christ. The American's enemy is his own fear and helplessness in the face of Vietnam. It is this fear and sense of impotence that makes the power used in his name all the more overwhelming and terrifying. This power, now swinging like a random scythe across a world in revolution whose humanity the American sees only dimly and fears greatly, is the primary locus of the Crucifixion in our time. A Catholic vision and commitment impels one to move out into the victims' path — turning one's face to the enemy who is ourselves — and to walk nonviolently with men in need against the opposite advance of what has become a virtually autonomous, murderous power. For it is this same power that can heal as well as kill mankind, and which will begin to do so only when the humanity of the "enemy" who is no enemy has begun to be acknowledged through a non-violent confrontation with him. The process of reconciliation can begin only when a Catholic vision — a recognition of the universal presence of Christ in man — has taken on life through a life in common with that human Christ who is naturally held most distant.

In the present situation Catholicism is an opening to the world as suffering, through one's specific commitment to the Vietnamese Christ. The suffering world, most of it dark of skin, feels its consciousness emerging through the cross of Vietnam. The execution is global. Technology not only murders with mass efficiency but it also makes the vision of that murder present to men's eyes everywhere. The vision of Vietnam's crucifixion has been burned into the eyes of mankind. The feeling for Vietnam is present wherever men have opened themselves as men to the reality of its cross, which is to say in most of the world. There is therefore offered through Vietnam a possible way of global redemption through a commitment to the humanity on that cross.

Vietnam has made vivid the crisis of power in a world where its possession is confined to a few who have no sense of global community. It is also making vivid the more profound power of men who have been born and raised in suffering, to endure suffering in war beyond any normal human limits and thereby to render impotent the destructive claims of weapons without limit. If the danger of genocide is raised, through an inexhaustible willingness to suffer and die on the one hand and to kill unrelentingly on the other, the redemptive possibilities of another course founded on such suffering is also suggested. If men today will suffer this much in war, and will meet daily tragedy with the kind of vibrant response evident in the people of North Vietnam, there is at least the possibility that some would suffer equally in peace for the creation of the global community that would prevent such wars. The virtually untapped power of humanity to resist inhumanity is evident even through the carnage of "one of the most barbarous wars in history" (U Thant). The reverse side of the war, however, raises the question as to just how much suffering America must inflict on the world before it becomes fully aware of the consequences of its fear, or worse, its indifference. Vietnam and its inevitable reflection in American cities moves one to confess that at this moment in history the hope of the world lies largely in a redemption of America from violence.

A Catholicism true to its name and willing to open itself to the world of suffering humanity epitomized in Vietnam must be a Catholicism of the Cross. To recognize suffering is to respond to it, and to respond to suffering is to take it on oneself. There is nothing sadistic or masochistic in Christ's imperative to take up one's cross in order to follow him. It is simply a realistic definition of love in a world where inhumanity challenges one constantly. A refusal to respond to the cross is a refusal to love, for man is on that cross and each of us has put him there. The center of the cross's presence today is Vietnam. A living belief in Christ in our time must therefore involve a recognition that napalm and cannister bombs are the contemporary forms of the nails that the Roman soldiers used.

The central affirmation of a Catholicism of the Cross is stated in the Vatican Council's *Constitution on the Church in the Modern World:*

> In our times a special obligation binds us to make ourselves the neighbor of every person without exception, and of actively helping him when he comes across our path, whether he be an old person abandoned by all, a foreign laborer unjustly looked down upon, a refugee, a child born of an unlawful union and wrongly suffering for a sin he did not commit, or a hungry person who disturbs our conscience by recalling the voice of the Lord, "As long as you did it for one of these the least of my brethren, you did it for me" (Matt. 25:40).

Few American Catholics have thought to apply this statement to the Viet Cong and the North Vietnamese. But without such application (where the inclination to make exceptions becomes most pressing) the statement is meaningless, as is Christ's reference to "these the least of my brethren." The American Church cannot respond to revolution in Vietnam because it has not begun to catch up to the meaning of the Catholic revolution.

On the other hand, Vietnam could act as a catalyst in the Church for an affirmation of true Catholicism and of that revolution of peace which is the Church's root meaning in Christ. There are growing signs of such a transformation of American Catholicism into a Catholicism of the Cross: the developing strength of the Catholic Peace Fellowship, the searching integrity of such publications as *Commonweal* and *The National Catholic Reporter,* most of all the formation everywhere of concerned communities of believers with the purpose of realizing in common precisely what it is they believe. These are small centers of concern in an American Church whose majority would probably vote to bomb Hanoi into the Stone Age. But the Church has always been an institution whose meaning and direction lay at its spiritual center. There is hope that if this core of concern can continue to grow in its testimony to the Vietnamese Christ, to the point of standing with him against the power of American violence, the Church in America may yet affirm the meaning of Catholicism.

9. The Bishops and Negotiation Now

Thomas Francis Ritt

THE AMERICAN HIERARCHY, WITH NOTABLE BUT FEW exceptions, has supported the war effort of the Johnson Administration. In lending their support to that effort they have supported American military intervention in the internal affairs of Vietnam.

In their annual statement of 1966 the American bishops said that U.S. presence in Vietnam could be morally justified. In 1967, at their annual meeting in Washington, the bishops adopted a resolution advocating negotiation, but did not repudiate their defense of armed intervention, which drew national headlines in 1966.

By the time their next meeting rolled around in April 1968, President Johnson had announced his intention not to run and talk of peace talks was in the air. The bishops found it possible once again to skirt the basic moral issues of the Vietnam war by expressing "grateful endorsement" of the President's decision "to limit the bombing of North Vietnam" and to seek negotiations. Since a moral judgment had evidently not been possible up to that point, they promised a joint pastoral letter within the year. This letter would address itself in part to the present critical problems of war and peace.

Although a layman may only speculate about the rationale of the bishops, I think it is becoming increasingly clear: as a corporate body the bishops continue to fuse the sacred and the secular. They do not seem aware of the subtle dangers to which they expose themselves in espousing a religious nationalism, a religion that seems to superimpose the cross on the flag in a manner that permits the nation — or its officials — to be the final arbiter of human affairs. The result is that the nation has a priority by which religion becomes not transcendent, but subservient to government.

The reasons for this obvious default are buried deep in our history. The American nation was born with a sense of national mission, a messianic hope enshrined in the Declaration of Independence and the Constitution. All through our history America has been the Promised Land. This is nowhere more evident in Catholic reaction to the war in Vietnam than in the remarks of the late Cardinal Spellman of New York while on a Christmas visit to American troops in Vietnam in 1966. As reported in a dispatch from Saigon published in *The New York Times,* the Cardinal was asked: "What do you think about what the United States is doing in Vietnam?" Answering that he "fully" supported "everything it does," the Cardinal para-phrased a nineteenth century naval hero: "My country may it always be right. Right or wrong, my country."

The Cardinal's statement was startling, and it disregarded the plain social teachings of recent popes as well as the guidelines set down in the *Constitution on the Church in the Modern World:* "It is our clear duty," said the Council Fathers in *Gaudium et Spes,* ". . . to strain every muscle as we work for the time when all war can be completely outlawed by interna-tional consent."

In a pamphlet published by the Center for the Study of Democratic Institutions, Robert Scheer makes it clear that he regards the late Cardinal as one of the prime movers of American involvement in Vietnam. This explains the Cardinal's reliance on Stephen Decatur and his support of Administration policy, perhaps, but we are left with the fact that almost the entire American episcopacy also supported that policy. We must look for the rationale if we are to understand the support.

The key to a proper understanding of the American bishops' support of the Vietnam war effort is, I think, the National Liberation Front, the political arm of the Viet Cong. The view that the bishops seem to have adopted is the view accepted by the government, namely, that Hanoi, a Communist regime in the North, gave orders to its followers in the South and that those orders were followed, leaving a civil war that was Communist-inspired. The National Liberation Front, then, was indistinguishable from Hanoi.

Secondly, our military presence in Vietnam was rationalized, at least initially, by the assumed existence of a monolithic Communism. This would influence the American hierarchy, but was best expressed, perhaps, by Secretary of State Dean Rusk. Just after taking office he said: "The central issue . . . is the announced determination to impose a world of coercion upon those not already subject to it . . . it is posed between the Sino-Soviet empire and all the rest, whether allied or neutral; and it is posed on every continent."

At the time this was political gospel. Americans by the millions, including hierarchy, accepted it as an infallible statement with the attendant need for action of a warlike nature in Vietnam. The Communists were threatening to take over!

Given this world view, it is not difficult to understand the commitment of the American bishops. In the early sixties Vatican II was but a dream of Pope John. An attitude of intransigence toward a monolithic Communism, almost forty years in the making, made it all but inevitable that the hierarchy would strongly support our involvement in Vietnam just as they supported the Marshall Plan and the Korean war. Communists, godless and tyrannical, were threatening the peace. They must be resisted.

The stage was set for war, for the horrendous spectacle of 100,000 casualties each year among the civilian population; for millions of Vietnamese homeless or displaced; for bombarding a small and weak nation with more firepower than was used in all of World War II; for the presence of more than a half million combat troops with the end still not in sight and for the expenditure of $100 billion. *Pax Americana* has become a frightening reality, but even with the whole arsenal of justifications we have engaged in a war that experts have said we cannot win.

Vietnam has become one of the major wars of the twentieth century. Undeclared, but divisive, spawning extremists on the Right and on the Left who seem intent on subverting our governmental system, it has become, finally, a dilemma for American Catholics. We have been and remain divided as never before by a war 10,000 miles from our shores.

All of this has had an impact on the American Catholic community. Impressive numbers of Catholics have learned to register dissent on an issue other than the traditional parochial ones. And for many the initial vehicle has been Negotiation Now. This national coalition for a political settlement of the war was launched in May 1967 and early attracted prestigious names. To almost everyone's surprise, American Catholic bishops were soon numbered among these.

The late Archbishop Paul Hallinan of Atlanta and Archbishop James Peter Davis of Santa Fe were probably the biggest names, but there were other early episcopal signers: James P. Shannon, auxiliary of St. Paul, John J. Dougherty, auxiliary of Newark and chairman of the Bishops' Committee on World Justice and Peace, Victor J. Reed, Bishop of Oklahoma City and Joseph P. Donnelly, auxiliary of New Haven.

Pittsburgh's Bishop John J. Wright, while not signing the initial petition, issued a statement commending the campaign, and his diocesan paper gave Negotiation Now its editorial endorsement.

What is it in the program of Negotiation Now that has made the breakthrough into the Catholic community? It has been best said by Archbishop Hallinan. In endorsing the campaign in July 1967, he wrote:

> It is probably inevitable that there are dozens of peace movements, and like demonstrations, these follow a sort of sociological law: Diminishing Returns. I am impressed in an entirely different way by Negotiation Now.
>
> There is a strong echo of Pope Paul's words in his 1966 Encyclical on Peace in Rabbi Heschel's phrase: "We can

commit ourselves unequivocally to seek *now* rather than *later* for a negotiated peace, realizing that history does not present us with easy choices." This is the kind of *realism* that everyone responsible for our national course must employ.

Negotiation Now incorporates another fresh approach. It clearly singles out "a kind of fatalism" in Michael Novak's words as the motivating force behind too much of our political, military and popular thinking. Negotiation Now proposes a healthy antidote to this fatalism. It offers action instead of hoping; "try a new path" instead of "more of the same." In rejecting this fatalism, our nation can regain its position for peace under God.

By then-current standards of anti-Vietnam protest, Negotiation Now was called moderate, even middle-class. Calling for an unconditional cessation of the bombing of North Vietnam as a first step, the campaign addressed itself to both combatant ideologies, stating it was not interested in fixing blame, but rather in finding a solution. According to spokesmen, the campaign was conscious of both Communist power and purpose. Assuming that the United States would take the first step, Negotiation Now then called for a standstill cease-fire and negotiations which, it contended, might lead to a political settlement of the war. The Achilles heel of the campaign, if one existed, was its insistence on free elections in *South* Vietnam and its growing hard-line anti-Communism.

Negotiation Now was launched in May, 1967, at a press conference in New York that featured the Reverend Martin Luther King, Jr. There are conflicting stories about its actual genesis, ranging from its being a child of SANE through that of its being the work of Robert Pickus, a long-time peace worker from California, aided by a group of militant Socialists in New York who shared Pickus's supposed hard-line anti-Communism. But whatever its beginnings, Negotiation Now has grown into a broad-based coalition and successfully made a significant breakthrough into the American Catholic community.

When the Catholic press began to headline the support of one bishop after another, it had the effect of somewhat muting the drumming of the siren "peace through strength" song that the military had been playing for so long. Bishops took a public stand for peace for the first time in the history of the American peace movement and they encouraged Catholic lay people to do the same. By early 1968, Negotiation Now had enlisted the support of significant numbers of American Catholics and, despite the negotiation overtures as this is written, the end is not yet. If the past is prologue, it is not inconceivable that American Catholics, numbering close to 50,000,000, might well become a major part of the future constituency of a continuing peace movement in the United States, particularly if the present polarization of thought in that movement continues to escalate.

Protest and dissent, when responsible and rational, has a way of proliferating, but its growth is dependent. In America, for example, even in these days of economic affluence, there are 22 million people considered functionally illiterate, not having completed the eighth grade. In this connection it seems likely that many of those millions are not likely to make subtle distinctions; they are susceptible to a continuation of the myth that we fight for freedom in Vietnam, or Laos, or wherever. The price we pay in depletion of our resources escapes them as we sustain and nurture the most gigantic "defense" budget in world history. Money and manpower continue to be poured into military and related work, creating, as Seymour Melman points out, a superabundance of killing power without precedent.

Imagine, for example, a Hiroshima-type bomb exploding every day of every year since the birth of Christ. Simple arithmetic tells us that the combined explosive force of all those bombs would be something like 14,000 megatons. The figure represents only 70 percent of the destructive power that the United States could deliver using only long-range bombers and missiles!

While it is true that increasing numbers in the Catholic community have seriously questioned our involvement in Vietnam, the majority apparently continue to support the war and would not resist its enlargement in order to "win." In short, Catholics divide on the issue no less than their fellow citizens. In his appearance before the Senate Foreign Relations Committee, former Ambassador George Kennan summed up the view of many on both sides of this tortuous issue when he said that American intervention in South Vietnam could not be justified, not even by the danger of complete Viet Cong control, "if it were not for the considerations of prestige that rise precisely out of our present involvement."

The question is then obvious: can Catholics continue to support military efforts that maim and kill many thousands of civilians every year because of "considerations of prestige"? The late Archbishop Hallinan provided an answer when he responded to members of his diocese who disapproved of his endorsement of Negotiation Now. Saying that the campaign he and other prelates endorsed was "well within the framework" of several Catholic documents, the Archbishop then added: "When I teach within the framework of a well-publicized Catholic position, I speak as a bishop and it would be faint-hearted to offer this merely as the view of a private citizen."

Nonetheless, Negotiation Now has been advisedly selective in seeking episcopal endorsement for the campaign. Even at this late date, for example, there are few American Catholics, and few members of the hierarchy, who are prepared to recognize the morally indefensible acts of the fire bombs on Tokyo, the obliteration bombing of European cities, or the use of the atom bomb on Hiroshima and Nagasaki. I am afraid there are too many who would accept without protest an H-bomb explosion over Hanoi, even though it is clear that the moral principles of the Gospels would never authorize it.

Still, believing that responsible dissent coupled with a positive and reasonable program to end the war would find fertile ground among the more reflective and progressive Catholics of episcopal rank, Negotiation Now has actively sought such support. As these efforts began to meet with some success, the campaign leaders came to realize that they were motivating something unprecedented in American peace activity.

In April, 1967, for example, Daniel Callahan published an article, "America's Catholic Bishops," in which he could write: "Though the American people are divided on the Vietnamese war, not one bishop has opposed it." The statement was true. However, as a result of the work of Negotiation Now, it was to be only a matter of weeks when the chairman of the newly created Bishops Committee for World Justice and Peace, the Most Rev. John J. Dougherty, became a national sponsor of the Negotiation Now Campaign. He was immediately followed, not only by other bishops, but by monsignori, priests, nuns, and laymen in ever increasing numbers. The "quiet, benign figure-heads" described by Mr. Callahan, became active against the war by taking a forthright stand that called for a negotiated, political settlement.

If many Catholics have been concerned before, Negotiation Now is the first broad and organized effort that large numbers have seen fit to support. Many other anti-war activities have seemed divisive. Negotiation Now is a large-scale voice of moderation and reason in an anti-war climate that has not been free of divisions that threaten to split the ranks of those interested in peace.

There is no gainsaying the fact that the peace movement comes in many pieces; it is customary, indeed, to say that it is hopelessly split. The October 1967 assault on the Pentagon, intended to pull together many of the diverse strands, succeeded only in dividing them further.

It is one thing to complain that many of the new militants in the anti-war movement are so "anti-American," believing that this society is rotten to the core, that they have foregone the chance of working within its framework. It is another to point out that an equally dangerous tendency seems to be developing now among the "responsible liberals," among some of the figures identified with Negotiation Now.

Just as I reject the militant's view that President Johnson was The Enemy, so do I resist the other view that Communism is The Enemy.

Many of these responsible liberals who have associated themselves with Negotiation Now are in danger of forgetting the Vietnamese history that pre-dates massive U.S. military involvement. There was a war in Vietnam that raged for eight years, from 1946 to 1954. And after that, elections, a *united* Vietnam, and peace were to come. But the United States, writes T. A. Bisson, Professor of International Studies at Western College for Women, "thought otherwise. And so American actions, first at Geneva and then at Saigon, stopped the election and there was no peace."

The settlement at Geneva in 1954, signed by the French and the Viet Minh, provided for two *temporary* zones along "a provisional *military* demarcation line" pending "general elections which will bring about the reunification of Vietnam." The Lawyers Committee on American Policy Towards Vietnam, including such legal authorities as Quincy Wright, Wolfgang Friedman, Thomas Emerson and Robert MacIver make it plain: ". . . indeed, under the Geneva Accords of 1954, South Vietnam is merely a temporary zone not even qualifying politically as a state."

These facts cannot easily be dismissed. They pose future problems for the growing coalition that is Negotiation Now. Will the bishops, for example, go along with the political direction of the campaign, which still calls for free elections in *South* Vietnam? Will the bishops and all the Catholics who support the movement continue to abide campaign literature that is highly selective and implicitly takes a rigid anti-Communist line? Can the United States continue to be classed with Hanoi as an armed ideology attempting to impose its will on the *South* Vietnamese by force of arms?

Despite the beginnings, in May 1968, of "peace talks," the campaign continues to grow. Attempts are being made to widen the coalition and to lessen the influence of the anti-Communists. John Kenneth Galbraith, for example, addressing a Washington meeting of Negotiation Now in June 1967, made it clear he believed it "salutary to search for error in one's past positions and attitudes."

"It was not," he continued, "the policy even in the most militant Cold War years to roll back the Communists from their established positions of power. Not even John Foster Dulles so urged."

Yet from personal and extended experience at the national level of Negotiation Now, I am afraid that such a position is not accepted by all. Some still passionately believe that the Viet Cong is an extension of Hanoi, and Hanoi, we are told in campaign literature, is one of two armed ideologies forcing its will on the people of the South.

What, then, is the future of Negotiation Now? Obviously, it is the heir apparent of SANE's former position as the largest peace group in the country. Not yet a membership organization, Negotiation Now has close to a million potential members and growing support in the Catholic community of nearly 50 million. Most of the support is for a negotiated, political settlement of the war and not for the perpetuation of a militaristic South Vietnam ruled by President Thieu and Vice-President Ky.

Yet in spite of the growing support, Negotiation Now is caught up in the raging fires of acrimonious debate within the peace movement. Parts of the staff, rigidly anti-Communist, have arbitrarily weeded out sponsors with whom political disagreement was envisioned. When Bishop Fulton J. Sheen of Rochester spoke out for withdrawal in the summer of 1967, Negotiation Now staff people were informed from on high that Bishop Sheen was not to be invited to become a sponsor. Others, like Msgr. Charles Owen Rice of Pittsburgh and Msgr. Joseph Gallagher of Baltimore, disappeared from the list of sponsors. Monsignor Rice had committed the unpardonable sin. He marched side by side with Dr. Benjamin Spock and supported the Fall Mobilization! Other Catholic supporters were dropped — or not used — because there were too many! There has been no further effort to involve other members of the hierarchy, even though this writer is almost certain that other bishops would support the campaign.

In short, it is my belief that the goals and political direction of Negotiation Now have been gradually but fundamentally altered by bureaucratic high-handedness and reflexive anti-Communism. It is my equally strong conviction that the thousands of Catholics who have supported Negotiation Now could prevent its goals from going by the board. When a parochial and rigid anti-Communism begins to appear, when a genuflection is made to the existence of two Vietnams and becomes a truth, when there is no mention of the Geneva Accords of 1954, when the *temporary* and *military* partition of the country is accepted as permanent and politically feasible, I would suggest that Catholics who support the campaign have an obligation to exert an influence that will correct these errors. It is time for Catholics to speak out — again!

10. The Catholic Press and Vietnam

John G. Deedy, Jr.

IN OCTOBER, 1967, THE GALLUP POLL RELEASED THE results of a survey showing that feeling in the country that the United States had made a mistake in sending troops to fight in Vietnam had almost doubled since August, 1965, rising from 24 percent to 46 percent. Gallup offered no breakdown of the degree to which the shift in opinion reflected itself in various groups or institutions, but the presumption is that it was pretty much general and averaged out.

Certainly Catholics are no exception to this presumption, if only minimal conclusions are drawn from the shift that has taken place in the Catholic Press. From near-unanimous firmness in the right of the American cause, Catholic Press opinion has moved to support for peace through negotiations to end the war. The change seems to have begun with the issuance by Pope Paul VI of his encyclical of October, 1966, *Christi Matri,* commemorating the first anniversary of his peace mission to the United Nations; it became the most pronounced as the futility of the Vietnam adventure impressed itself on the consciences of growing numbers of Americans.

This is not to suggest that the Catholic Press is markedly less superpatriotic than before, nor more supranationally humanitarian — only that it is somewhat more realistic about the impasse that is the Vietnam war, more aware of the implications of the fighting in terms of the possibility of a wider world war, and, finally, sensitive at last to the peace pleas of Pope Paul. Even so, it remains a nationalist press standing in great awe of

121

duly constituted political authority. Indeed, on the question of Vietnam, until *Christi Matri,* the Catholic Press seemed far more receptive to the persuasions of the Administration than the pleadings of the papacy. Of only a few Catholic publications is this true today, but some do exist.

All of which is to say that, though generalization is possible in evaluating the performance of the Catholic Press on the Vietnam war issue, allowance must still be made for considerable variance within that generalization.

Clear evidence of the failure of the Catholic Press to fit into a neat, single category is provided by the diocesan press:

— There are the hawks, like the Los Angeles *Tidings,* strong on the domino and "better dead than red" theories and *The Guardian* of the Diocese of Little Rock, which sees the war as part of a holy crusade against Communism ("At the present time, the forces of evil are at work on all sides, threatening the destruction of civilization. It is well known that the Communists are at work, not only in such places as Vietnam, but even in our own country in many important departments of government. The American people seem to be unaware of the widespread activities of Communism or they are fools enough to think that it can't happen here . . .").

— There are the doves, like the *Catholic Voice* of Oakland, California, which urged, before most others, cessation of bombing of North Vietnam and gradual withdrawal from South Vietnam, and the *St. Louis Review,* which saw the war rendering the United States virtually friendless in a hostile world and increasingly prone to violence at home ("We must pursue peace through negotiation more intently and openly and honestly than we have in the past. We must do this with every resource and through agencies such as the UN and the Vatican. We must offer the olive branch without brandishing the sword at the same time").

— And there are the middle-ground publications, those who hear the peace pleas of Pope Paul but who speak in the accents of the majority of American bishops, and accordingly offer a program so qualified that all — those opposed to the war as well as those who favor it — are able to find justification for their positions. The Chicago *New World's* editorial on *Christi Matri* provides an example of how some diocesan publications can take a peace message and blunt it with qualifiers and rationalizations. *The New World* editorialized in October of 1966:

> The Vicar of Christ . . . is calling for a peace that will "rest on justice and the liberty of mankind and take into account the rights of individuals and communities." These words express quite clearly the position our nation has been following. We are not in Vietnam for any national or personal gain. Our President has offered more than once to settle the affair by reasonable conferences. The Communists — the Viet Cong, the Red Chinese, the Soviets and the whole puppet Soviet bloc — have consistently refused to cooperate. For the United States to capitulate to Communist demands for the cessation of warfare under their terms would be not only "shifting and unstable" to use the words of the Holy Father; it would be fatal to world freedom and ruinous to any hope for true peace.

It may be unfair to *The New World* to cite its 1966 editorial, since almost a year to the day later *The New World* had come virtually full circle and was editorializing in favor of cessation of American bombing raids so as to contribute to a climate in which negotiations could take place. But, with all credit to *The New World* for its new enlightenment, that 1966 editorial does demonstrate a common condition: the penchant in the Catholic Press to equivocate on the moral responsibilities and implications of Vietnam. This is not so strange as on quick thought it may seem. If individual bishops are determinants in the orientation of diocesan newspapers — as, of course, they are — it is quite understandable. For on Vietnam the American bishops, by and large, have set a style for equivocation, beginning with their collective statement of 1966. Then there are individual examples. Recall Cardinal Lawrence Shehan's attempt in June, 1966, to measure the Vietnam war against the principles enunciated in Vatican II's *Constitution on the Church in the Modern World;* both hawks and doves were able to claim it for support (when he thought peace people had gone too far in their claims, Cardinal Shehan issued a clarification that reduced the statement to absolute innocuousness). Recall, too, how few bishops would sign the relatively non-controversial Negotiation Now petition, one that would take them no appreciable distance in their peace position beyond the statements of Pope Paul and that was in effect endorsed by the Administration in its seeming willingness to begin peace talks in Spring 1968. Only a handful had signed the Negotiation Now petition eight months after it had been around, and the signatures of many American bishops had been individually solicited. The point is obvious: given the measure by which bishops help set the tone of the diocesan press, it is small wonder that episcopal indecisiveness on the war in Vietnam should be reflected in diocesan newspapers.

But it cannot be said that each and every diocesan newspaper is the mirror of the local bishop's mind on Vietnam; quite the contrary. In Pittsburgh, Bishop John J. Wright at first declined to sign the Negotiation Now statement because it did not address itself to "the systematic murder by agents of the Viet Cong of potential intellectual and political leaders of South Vietnam or any eventually reunited nation"; however, the *Pittsburgh Catholic,* in the same issue reporting Bishop Wright's reservation (under the awkward head "Bishop Hedges Endorsement of Peace Group"), endorsed Negotiation Now without qualification. "Its literature, its representatives and its stated policy reveal it to be a reasoned and reasonable attempt to bridge the ever-widening understanding gap between the doves and the hawks," said the *Pittsburgh Catholic.* In St. Paul, on the other hand, Auxiliary Bishop James P. Shannon wrote enthusiastically of Negotiation Now in the diocesan newspaper, *The Catholic Bulletin,* seeing its proposals as a reasonable middle course between the extremes of unilateral withdrawal and continued escalation; however, editor Bernard Casserly wrote on the page facing Bishop Shannon's endorsement: "we cannot in conscience urge you to support it."

Casserly's objections were bound up with imputations about American sincerity and certain pragmatic military considerations. But they are not important to the point of the St. Paul and the Pittsburgh situations; that is, the diocesan press resists blanket categorization not only as a communications unit but also as the reflection of the mind of the bishop(s) in the diocese in which it publishes; there is a range of opinion in the publications as well as among bishops and editors. Nevertheless, the St. Paul and the Pittsburgh cases demonstrate that differences, where they occur publicly, are not substantive, nor are they sufficient to place bishops or diocesan press markedly to the right or left of one another. If, as a body, one is more or less irresolute, so is the other — with exceptions noted: among the bishops, the late Archbishop Paul Hallinan of Atlanta, Bishop Fulton Sheen of Rochester, Bishop Shannon and two or three more; among the diocesan newspapers, the *St. Louis Review,* the *Oklahoma Courier,* the *Delmarva Dialog,* the *Catholic Star Herald* of Camden, the *Pittsburgh Catholic* and a few others.

The *Pittsburgh Catholic,* incidentally, is an interesting study in editorial adventuresomeness. Over the years (going back before this writer's editorship there), *Pittsburgh Catholic* editorials have often been reprinted in *The Worker,* the publication of the Communist Party in the U.S. Also, *Pittsburgh Catholic* columnist Msgr. Charles Owen Rice has been quoted more than a few times by Hanoi Radio and other Communist outlets. But, admittedly, one publication does not determine the character of the diocesan press, any more than do lay-edited independents like *The National Catholic Reporter* and *Commonweal* — both outspoken opponents of the war in Vietnam — determine the character of the Catholic Press as a whole. At most, they dramatize the diversity of opinion which is possible within the Catholic Press.

Because the Catholic Press publications that pursue policies of dissent have traditionally been quality publications in the currents of progressive change, their positions are sometimes mistaken by the unknowledgeable as being more representative than they actually are of Catholic thought in general. The fact is that on Vietnam, as on controverted questions of the past, the liberal voice in the Catholic Press is a lonely one. The bulk of support is historically on the side of authority. So far as

Vietnam is concerned, this would place the Catholic Press for peace, but on terms understood and defined by authority — in this case the Administration.

Certainly the writings of Rev. Patrick O'Connor, the correspondent covering the war in Vietnam for NC News Service, the bishops' official news agency, are on the side of the Administration.

Despite competition from Religious News Service, an agency of the National Conference of Christians and Jews, NC dominates news services reports in the Catholic Press. Invariably, therefore, the O'Connor dispatches enjoy a predominance when it comes to Vietnam. The problem is that Father O'Connor is so anti-Communist and pro-American (he himself is a native of Ireland) that his writings have a ring about them of U.S. State Department propaganda; also, he is committed to the "Catholic-angle" view of the news, so that a distortion immediately crops up in his reports, making it seem as though the big story in Vietnam is how the war affects Catholic missionaries, Catholic institutions, Catholic programs, Catholic political personalities, Catholic villages, Catholic soldiers, Catholic anything. Floyd Anderson, director of NC News Service, considers Father O'Connor an "excellent correspondent"; so do many Catholic Press editors. But not all editors are so persuaded. Most editors concede Father O'Connor's experience and knowledge-ableness about the Far East, but not a few distrust his reporting because of the intensity of his biases. One editor says privately, "I have a prejudice against Father Patrick O'Connor to the extent that I almost refuse to print anything with his byline." The problem is that there is hardly any other choice; it's O'Connor or no one. NC also has a Father Patrick Burke, like O'Connor, a Columban Father, writing from Vietnam, but he is more or less a "back-up," the man who will take over full coverage when Father O'Connor, no longer young or in the best of health, leaves Vietnam. So if one refuses to take Father O'Connor, there is RNS or nothing. RNS is a very competent and reliable agency, but its coverage out of Vietnam, accurate though it may be, has been routine. It is a reflection on NC and

Father O'Connor that many editors prefer RNS's routine coverage to the heavier-investment, man-on-the-scene reporting of NC's Father O'Connor.

Unfortunately, costs are such that Catholic publications cannot afford the luxury of covering the war with reporters of their own. Only *The National Catholic Reporter* has sent a correspondent to Vietnam, and it did so at financial investment it could ill afford. Still, it was an investment that was worth while, comments editor Robert Hoyt, in summing up the assignment of Michael Novak to Vietnam for several weeks in the summer of 1967. "His story about American Catholic Relief Services' involvement in supporting the Popular Forces of South Vietnam [a story that brought a storm of rebuttal amounting to overkill] made the whole thing worth the effort," Hoyt remarked recently. Catholic Press editors followed Mr. Novak's reporting with envy as well as professional interest, and for not a few editors it confirmed that more intelligent and more valid insights into the war are possible, even from a parochial platform, than those propagandized by Father O'Connor.

Curiously, few among the Catholic Press reading public appear to be the least bit distressed by the Administration-programmed reporting of Father O'Connor. But let Catholic Press columnists be anti-Administration and they quickly discover where sentiments are strongest among rank-and-file Catholics. Donald McDonald, a columnist and former editor who fought the good fight during the McCarthy era and took his lumps because of his uncompromising stance, finds history repeating itself. In two years, from 1965-1967, McDonald has seen his client papers drop from ten to five. Not all the cancellations can be traced directly to his anti-war views, but some can. One priest-editor, in notifying McDonald of his discontinuance, said: "I will be frank and tell you the reason we are dropping [the column] is because I disagree with your views on Vietnam." Father John Sheerin, C.S.P., editor of the *Catholic World,* who is syndicated through NC News Service, has likewise encountered difficulties. He has lost several papers, and is likely to lose more as a consequence of his aligning himself with those advocating civil disobedience and publicly counselling young men "who in conscience cannot today serve in the armed forces to refuse such service by non-violent means."

Like McDonald, Father Sheerin declines to attribute all his client cancellations to antipathy to his views on the war in Vietnam. Stop orders, he concedes, are usually abrupt and generally offer no explanations. Still, Father Sheerin is persuaded that the *Texas Catholic's* dropping of his column results from his position on Vietnam, and there are others about whose decision he has legitimate suspicions.

On the other hand, Father Sheerin is unconvinced that cancellations are a completely accurate gauge to the attitudes of editors. "Generally," he remarked, "if an editor doesn't like your column, he just skips it."

It may be worth pointing out that a diocesan editor, largely dependent on NC News for other than local copy, is not restricted just to O'Connor's hawkish dispatches and Sheerin's dovish columns. NC has given generally good coverage to what might be called "religious comment" on the war — protest demonstrations by seminarians, pastoral letters of Bolivian, Mexican, or French bishops decrying the war, anti-Vietnam resolutions passed by Catholic organizations, and so on. A few papers, such as *The Catholic Virginian,* have been able to paste together some strong anti-war editorials merely by rounding up the week's news.

As might be predicted, the two mass-audience weeklies of the Catholic Press, *The Register* and *Our Sunday Visitor* (each with circulations over 750,000) have made no appreciable contribution to the clarification of the issues involved in Vietnam. Traditionally nationalist and conservative, both papers have responded to the challenge of Vietnam in fashion consistent with their history: the American cause being automatically supportable and the opposition cause, particularly since it smacks of Communism, being suspect.

It is hardly an accident of fate that the conservative answer to *The National Catholic Reporter,* the new independent weekly, *Twin Circle,* should have drawn its two principal personalities from *The Register* and the *Visitor:* Frank Morriss and Daniel Lyons, S. J. Morriss was news editor and a reactionary columnist at *The Register;* Father Lyons, a hawk who can outfly all hawks, appeared as a columnist in *Our Sunday Visitor.* After Vietnam mushroomed, he became to *Visitor* readers what Father Richard Ginder was to its readers of the McCarthy era.

With Lyons and Morriss gone from *Our Sunday Visitor* and *The Register,* observers are genuinely hopeful that both publications will take new directions, particularly as the new editors of each — Msgr. Vincent A. Yzermans at *Our Sunday Visitor* and Father Daniel Flaherty at *The Register* — continue to make their presence felt. Both are men of enlightened, progressive reputations.

If the diocesan press picture is mixed, no less so is that of the Catholic magazine press. Many of these are monthly or bi-monthly periodicals, and thus have the very real problem of topicality; in addition some do not have formal editorial departments. But quality publications among Catholic magazines still manage to quicken consciences on the war issue. *Jubilee* is a case in point. Though a monthly that at least until recently did not carry editorials, *Jubilee* has been able to convey a sense of urgency over the war in Vietnam, through an orientation under editor Edward Rice that was consistently dovish. *Jubilee* changed owner and editorship in August, 1967, but its commitment to peace has continued, if occasionally confused by ambiguous "editorials" boxed as signed feature columns.

The Critic, Catholic World, U.S. Catholic, Sign, and *Ave Maria* have also kept readers alert to the implications of American involvement in Vietnam by periodically scrutinizing the political and moral issues involved in the conflict. *Ave Maria,* for example, made what was perhaps the sharpest attack on the American Catholic Relief Services' operation in South Vietnam. Summing up the reporting of other journals, *Ava Maria* focused on CRS's tie-in with the American military establishment and urged readers to withhold contributions to the American relief agency and give instead through Caritas Internationalis, a

Vatican-based organization that distributes aid irrespective of national allegiances.

U.S. Catholic, a once-moribund family magazine published by the Claretian Fathers and called *The Voice of St. Jude,* carried one of the most thoughtful and detailed editorials to come out of the Vietnam war in its December 1967 issue. It resulted, predictably enough, in the greatest spate of letters the magazine has ever received. I don't think it is just my own bias or the selective printing by the editors which suggests that the letters fell neatly into two categories. Most opposed were typical crank letters of outrage, calling the editors Communists and ending with the ritual "cancel my subscription," while many of the favorable letters (surprisingly, a majority, at least of those printed) were unusually sensitive and informed; some helpfully carried the editorial position into new areas of consideration.

As for the big opinion-makers in the Catholic magazine field, *Commonweal* and *America,* they are divided on the issue of Vietnam. *America,* to the disappointment of many who would expect of a Jesuit publication an unconditional commitment to peace, is firmly in the camp of the hawks: "We are in Vietnam for either or both of two main reasons. The first, which many intelligent and reputable dissenters from Administration policy deem arguable, is that our presence in Southeast Asia is essential to our national security. The second, which is not arguable, is that we are there to prevent 17 million Vietnamese from being swallowed up by a voracious and aggressive Communism" (Sept. 23, 1967). Lay-edited *Commonweal,* on the other hand, has not only branded the war indecent and immoral, but has endorsed the escalation of dissent to the level of civil disobedience:

> The resistance envisioned is a passive disobedience in the tradition of Thoreau. This might take the form of withholding of taxes, counseling, aiding or abetting young men on avoidance of the draft . . . , or disruption tactics of various sorts. Such conduct might sound extreme to some, but, as Robert McAfee Brown writes in a recent issue of *Look,* the war is so wrong, and ways of registering concern about it have

become so limited, that civil disobedience is the only course left.

By so editorializing, *Commonweal* became the first (October, 1967) Catholic publication to take a stand in favor of civil disobedience as a legitimate form of anti-war protest — excepting, of course, the *Catholic Worker,* which traditionally has been pacifist but anarchist in its pursuit of pacifist principles.

But after all is said and done, the essential problem with Catholic newspapers and magazines, including many dove publications of high reputation, is that they fail to convey the same sense of urgency on the question of peace that they do on matters of considerably lesser importance. If pope or bishops issue a peace statement, the Catholic Press can be counted upon to play the news story prominently and very likely back it up with an affirming editorial. But frequently these turn out to be "one-shot" efforts. The following week most publications can be counted upon to be back on the tried-and-true topics that are the staples of a parochial press — development fund drives, the liturgical calendar, legislative issues affecting Catholic interests, questions of public morality, etc. No one disputes that these subjects merit the attention of a religious press. What is arguable is the preoccupation with those topics to the neglect, reportorial and editorial, of what should be the basic Christian concern — peace among men. It is this inversion of priorities that ultimately constitutes the strongest indictment against the Catholic Press. It is an indictment that only few Catholic publications escape.

11. War in the Parish

WILLIAM F. NERIN

WHEN OUR INVOLVEMENT IN VIETNAM HAS COST US
2 to 3 billion dollars a month; when thousands of American
boys and hundreds of thousands of Vietnamese have been
killed; when our original stated policy of the war's being a
Vietnamese war has turned to its being our war, and our longest
war since the Revolution; when the opinion of mankind for
which we are supposed to have a decent respect is largely turned
against us; when the massive social problems at home of
poverty and racism still go unmet; when our slums fester in-
human conditions; when Congress is unwilling to appropriate
money to attack these local injustices; when conscientious
objectors today outnumber their Korean War counterparts four
to one; when there is more controversy over our involvement in
this war than during any other conflict since the Civil War; when
the freedoms of peoples are at stake; when the real possibility
exists of escalation into a third world war and nuclear bombing
— then it is reasonable to assume that our engagement in
Vietnam constitutes a crucial moral question.

Certainly for the Catholic pastor, the morality of this question
has been heightened by the actions and statements of Pope
Paul VI. And since pastors are supposed to be religious leaders,
they should come to grips with the morality of the war and thus
help their people in the formation of conscience. The memory
of the German church and German Catholics during the Nazi
regime is all too fresh in our minds for us not to take a lesson
from that experience. But the available evidence seems to

indicate an alarming absence of serious concern within the
American Church, on all levels, with a vital moral question that
is pondered and debated and agonized over in almost every
other element of American society. Perhaps one thing is more
alarming than the lack of meaningful discussion of the war's
morality within the parish community: that is the fact that few
seem to expect such discussion.

What is the pastor to do? Obviously, he should first rethink
his priorities. He must at least begin to acquaint himself with
the complexities of the issues involved in the Vietnam situation.
Literature, easily available, and much of it directed to the moral
and ethical aspects, abounds. Anyone claiming to be an informed citizen must read, but a moral leader has a special
responsibility to go beyond the editorial page of the local daily.

Then, he must talk with people about the issues; and "talk"
means listening much of the time. I have found it helpful to
talk with servicemen returned from Vietnam, an opportunity
present to most clergymen. All shades of opinion are exhibited,
from disgust, disillusionment, and firm opposition to the American presence in Vietnam to an almost unqualified enthusiasm for
"the cause."

One can talk also with civilians who have been in Vietnam,
newsmen and relief workers. In my own experience, these have
been among the most helpful in trying to get a perspective on
the situation.

Read, listen, then judge; at least attempt to weigh the known
facts against whatever moral criteria one has. And the pastor
must depend not only on the traditional formulas of the
Church's teaching on war but especially on the current thinking
of contemporary Christian theologians.

Then he must stimulate thought within the congregation.
This is probably the most difficult part, or so it would seem,
given the fact that most Catholic parishes have apparently not
provided for such discussion within parochial structures. But it
is not really such a difficult task; if the pastor is open and non-
dogmatic about it, the congregation will be too. This is how the
Community of John XXIII in Oklahoma City went about it.

At one Sunday meeting, two men, prepared to speak on opposite sides of the issue, started off the discussion, which was followed by questions, challenges, and additional information from the floor. After an hour and a half of this, we took a straw vote. The vote revealed that only a very few had still not made up their minds. In John XXIII about half took a position resembling that of the Administration at the time, and half took an opposing stand. From this we decided to form a Hawk Committee and a Dove Committee, each to prepare a position paper for its group. The papers were prepared and used as a further educational device within the community so that as events have changed we have been able to rethink our stands on the issues.

Another example is offered by a Methodist Church in Oklahoma City that conducted a series of lectures and discussions on the Vietnam situation on Sunday evenings, again presenting both sides. There are obviously many approaches to this basic task of stimulating people to be concerned about the critical issues facing our world and to form mature judgments. The Church has to become a forum for concern and decision in matters that are vital to its own reason for existing.

In all such matters, it is essential that the pastor exude a spirit of freedom. The people must form their own personal consciences. It should be made very clear that because the issues are so complex, total agreement or consensus will be unlikely if not impossible.

To respect the freedom of the people, the pastor and the people themselves should respect each other in working toward the positions they form within their own consciences. If those who are doves wish to support certain peace movements (as I was active, for example, in Negotiation Now) the hawks should respect this. If the hawks want to work toward the support of the present Administration policy, the doves must respect them in their efforts. This requires the deepest sort of Christian respect for one's fellow man. It requires a balanced inner security and certainly a sense of humor. It requires that each side know that the other is honestly motivated and striving for a Christian response.

In all of this the role of the pastor is to make sure that he and his people try to investigate both sides of the question; that the moral principles are brought clearly forth in order that a judgment might be made; that civility, facts, and reason are present; and that some attempt be made to probe more deeply into the theology of the gospel as it may apply to this situation.

If this approach is made, we will also be providing for our people the emotional release that they need in order to live in a healthy way with those who disagree with them. This is not to deny the seriousness and importance of the issues and the influence one's formed conscience should have on one's life, but rather it is to recognize that we cannot force our views on others.

There is one particular responsibility of today's pastors that has been little recognized. As a friend and counselor of many young people in his parish (and of their anxious parents), a pastor must deal with the question of conscientious objection. He must be familiar not only with the clear teaching of Vatican II on this matter (which is, after all, only the traditional view on the inviolability of an informed conscience applied to the modern fact of universal conscription); he must also apprise himself of the present legal situation regarding the draft.

Basic here is a Christian awareness, in pastor and people, that conscience must be obeyed before government. People must come to appreciate the Church's veneration of conscientious objectors as heroes and saints. The example of Saint Thomas More stands before us today; the dramatic presentation in "A Man for All Seasons" has made many of us aware of the painful dilemmas the Christian must confront when he passes beyond simple slogans and superficial religion. Here, too, the opinions voiced shortly before his death by John Courtney Murray are important for pastors and young Catholic men in particular. Murray argued strongly that the present laws must be changed to allow alternative, non-military service for those who, while they are not pacifists, cannot support a particular war such as that in Vietnam. In all, the pastor must make it terribly clear what the moral implications are when the young decide their relation to the military.

An alert pastor, finally, will warn against imputing bad motives to those who take different points of view. Where national pride is involved, as in this case, it can become tragically easy to impugn as unpatriotic those who disagree with the Administration. The clergyman's role here is to prick the bubble of exaggerated nationalism which, in time of crisis, goes under the proud name of patriotism. He must point out that within our very framework of government the most patriotic person is he who voices his honest opinion even though it is a dissenting one. In a democracy such as ours it is unpatriotic for a dissenter not to express his dissent.

Does this hold true for the pastor of a parish, for the bishop of a diocese? I believe it does. Priests and bishops, perhaps especially because of the public nature of their ministry, but certainly because of their role as moral leaders, should bear public witness to their convictions. They are not to put forth their convictions as gospel truth, nor pretend they are speaking for the Church when they are only speaking *from* the Church, articulating a Christian view with which other Christians may legitimately disagree. But they must speak.

A pastor's position is a difficult one; he will have parishioners, often a majority, who will disagree with him; he will have others who are still too quickly influenced by anything "Father says." But the conscientious pastor will speak and witness to his convictions. He will do so even — perhaps especially — in the pulpit, with a great consciousness of the respect he must have for others, with still greater consciousness of the respect he must have for the truth, and with a great humility.

12. No Longer Alone: The Catholic Peace Movement

JAMES H. FOREST

"ONE NEVER NEEDS ANY MONEY TO START A GOOD work. People are what count. If you have the people and they are willing to give their work, God will not be outdone in generosity. The funds will come in somehow or other."

The words were Peter Maurin's spoken to Dorothy Day in late December, 1932. The two had only recently met and already were in the process of founding what the world now knows as the Catholic Worker movement. Neither had any money. There were no wealthy backers. Had it not been for Peter's conviction that "funds will come in somehow or other" very likely there would have been no Catholic Worker movement. And if it is true that for want of a nail, a battle is lost, it many be said that neither would there have been a Catholic peace movement such as exists today — certainly nothing as well formed and visible, and even slightly respectable.

Deservedly, the story of the Catholic Worker's founding has become almost legendary. Dorothy Day, a recent convert to Catholicism, once a socialist journalist and editor, had gone to Washington to cover the Hunger March for *Commonweal*, a progressive lay-edited Catholic weekly. The march, largely because of its Communist-backing, had inspired considerable governmental hostility as well as scare headlines in the press. After weeks of travel, tear-gassed public meetings, and much police brutality, the band of unemployed workers, numbering in the thousands, reached Washington's city limits. For days they were held at gunpoint, finally being permitted to march to the Capitol steps to personally petition government action and assistance.

Dorothy Day later wrote:

> I stood on the curb and watched them, joy and pride in the courage of this band of men and women mounting in my heart, and with it a bitterness, too, that since I was now a Catholic, with fundamental philosophical differences, I could not be out there with them. I could write, I could protest, to arouse the conscience, but where was the Catholic leadership in the gathering of bands of men and women together, for the actual works of mercy that the comrades had always made part of their technique in reaching the worker?

That had happened on an icy December day, the 8th, the Feast of the Immaculate Conception. After leaving the march route, she went to the Shrine of the Immaculate Conception, then still under construction. In its crypt church — which can perhaps be thought of as the birthplace of the Catholic Worker — she offered up a "special prayer": "I offered up a special prayer, a prayer which came with tears and with anguish, that some way would open for me to use what talents I possessed for my fellow workers, for the poor."

She met Peter Maurin for the first time the next day, upon returning to her railroad flat on East 15th Street, Manhattan.

Peter Maurin, then 57, was hardly the most "impressive" sort of man, in his dusty, unpressed, ill-fitting suits, pockets bulging with booklets. Still, as Dorothy would relate later, he didn't look like a fanatic. "He was good as bread," she thought, "a truly happy man, with the happiness a man feels when he has found his true vocation in life and has set out on the way and is sure of himself."

Their backgrounds had been very different. Peter, born in the south of France, had been one of many children and was raised in communal simplicity; an ancient Christian cultural heritage was in the air he breathed. After years as a teaching Christian Brother, he found his way to Canada, then the U.S., where he farmed and wandered, sometimes working as a day laborer, sometimes trading room and board for French lessons. He was a voracious reader and incessant lecturer. Despite his thick accent, his manner of presentation — full of easily remembered phrases and images — quickly impressed his message in the listener's memory. His words, put in writing in blank verse form, came to be known as "easy essays":

> The world would be better off, if people tried to become better.
> And people would become better, if they stopped trying to be better off.

The disciples that were later to form around him at the Catholic Worker knew many of Peter's essays by heart and could quickly join in the litany:

> For when everybody tries to be better, everybody is better off.
> Everybody would be rich if nobody tried to become richer.
> And nobody would be poor if everybody tried to be the poorest.
> And everybody would be what he ought to be if everybody tried to be what he wants the other fellow to be.

His genius was to take the outrageous core of the Christian message and put it in a way that compelled attention and even retention. For those who thought Christianity of its nature required obscure presentations, Peter could be an electrifying experience.

Christian culture was *not* in the air in which Dorothy Day was raised. Born in 1896, she had lived in various parts of the U.S. — San Francisco, Chicago, New York. As a student she was caught up in the radical momentum of pre-World War I America, and drawn into socialism. Leaving school and family for New York, she worked for a socialist daily, lived in tenements, interviewed the notable radicals of her day, including Leon Trotsky. With thousands of others, she celebrated news of the Russian Revolution at a thunderous Madison Square Garden rally. Elizabeth Gurly Flynn, then a Wobbly, one day to serve as a leader of the American Communist Party, won Dorothy's friendship at an early date because of her devotion to jobless miners in Kentucky. (Up to the time of Gurly Flynn's death, she would send blankets and old clothes to the Catholic Worker's house of hospitality, St. Joseph's in New York.)

Dorothy had the additional credentials of having served a prison term for picketing the White House in a suffrage demonstration. Several years later, while staying in a Wobbly community apartment in Chicago, she was again arrested, this time in the famous Palmer raids.

Five years prior to meeting Peter Maurin, Dorothy passed through the most definitive phase of her life, her conversion to Catholicism. She had been married to a beach-combing anarchist, with whom she lived in a Staten Island cottage looking out over the bay. His distaste for religion was such that when she was received into the Church, he felt compelled to leave. Dorothy supported herself and her daughter, Tamar, by magazine work, proceeds from a novel and a brief stint as a Hollywood scriptwriter, finally returning to New York's Lower East Side, to share an apartment with her sister and her journalist husband.

The collaboration made possible by the meeting of Peter Maurin and Dorothy Day produced a first issue of *The Catholic Worker* just in time for May Day, 1933, when 2500 copies of the first small issue were distributed at the massive gathering at Union Square.

The first editorial began, simply, TO OUR READERS:

> For those who are sitting on park benches in the warm spring sunlight.
> For those who are huddling in shelters trying to escape the rain.
> For those who are walking the streets in the all but futile search for work.
> For those who think that there is no hope for the future, no recognition of their plight — this little paper is addressed.
> It is printed to call their attention to the fact that the Catholic Church has a social program — to let them know that there are men of God who are working not only for their spiritual, but for their material welfare.
> It's time there was a Catholic paper printed for the unemployed. The fundamental aim of most radical sheets is the conversion of its readers to Radicalism and Atheism.

Is it not possible to be radical and not atheist?

Is it not possible to protest, to expose, to complain, to point out abuses and demand reforms without desiring the overthrow of religion?

In an attempt to popularize and make known the encyclicals of the Popes in regard to social justice and the program put forth by the Church for the "reconstruction of the social order," this news sheet, *The Catholic Worker,* is started.

By the end of its first years, *The Catholic Worker* had become an attractive, eight-page tabloid monthly with a circulation of 100,000. By 1936, it was 150,000; by 1938, 165,000.

The Catholic Worker had both immediate and long-range interests — an immediate concern with the alleviation of human suffering, and a long-range ambition to rebuild society in such a way, as Peter Maurin put it, "that it would be easier for man to be human."

In order to serve immediate needs, the house of hospitality idea was put forward. "We need houses of hospitality," Peter announced in the *Worker's* pages, "in order to give the rich an opportunity to serve the poor."

The first such hospice was born when a young, pregnant, and unemployed woman came into the *Worker's* editorial office, which until recently had been the place of business for the organ-grinder barber who worked at the street level just beneath Dorothy's apartment.

The young woman took charge of the kitchen and started cooking for the homeless persons already drifting in the front door. "It wasn't long before we were all eating in shifts," Dorothy recalls.

As a step toward what Peter called "the green revolution," communities were begun on the land — combination farms and schools, with the added function of providing hospitality. It was Peter's hope that "a worker-scholar synthesis" could be achieved within farming communities. In the midst of the Depression, Peter was glad to remind any who would listen, "There is no unemployment on the land!" The words often served as a headline in the *Worker's* pages.

With the rise of Hitler in Europe, the question of war was introduced to the *Worker's* pages at an early date, first with a 1934 editorial reminding readers of the Church's just war doctrine, followed shortly afterward with an imaginary debate between Christ and a Patriot. (It was written by Paul Hanly Furfey, still a pacifist, now a Monsignor of the Church and distinguished author-sociologist based at Catholic University.) Jesus Christ, Furfey wrote, though living in an occupied nation controlled by pagans, opposed those who advocated violent and nationalist solutions to Roman presence and control.

One could say that it was with that single article that the American Catholic peace movement was born.

Along with *Commonweal, The Catholic Worker* refused to lend its support to Franco's "holy war" in Spain. For its stand — seen by the rest of the Catholic press and most of the hierarchy as complicity with Communism — the *Worker* was expelled from the Catholic Press Association. (In later years, when grass roots murmur had elected Dorothy a saint, the *Worker* was invited back into the CPA, but turned it down.)

Though some who were active with the houses of hospitality volunteered for military service, the *Worker* persisted with its pacifism throughout World War II.

Predictably, it took a subscription beating for its stand, but owing to its continuing commitment to nonviolence, discussions occurred with the Church which proved to be of enormous historical importance: Is a just war a continuing or realistic possibility, if one takes seriously the limitations demanded by Augustinian and Thomistic schools of theology? To what extent is a Christian expected to embrace sanctity and the counsels of perfection? (Some then argued it was sufficient to believe dogma, go to mass and contribute to the Church.) What is the basis for Catholic conscientious objection? Can bullets serve as emissaries of Christ's liberation? And on and on.

If the Catholic Worker had been only a newspaper, its concern with peace and nonviolence would have been of lesser import. Coupled, however, with its houses of hospitality and concern with voluntary poverty, a new variety of Christian began to emerge — perhaps even a new kind of person, and many of the magazine's readers were not Catholic and often not even churchgoers.

Certainly the Catholic Worker represented a significant break with the left, in terms of the new movement's dual emphasis on radical action *and* immediate commitment to the traditional works of mercy: feeding the hungry, housing the homeless, caring for the sick, visiting the prisoner, and so forth. The dual emphasis was eventually adopted by many in the New Left.

It is true that for more than thirty years there was veritably no other Catholic organization that provided support to Catholic conscientious objectors or seriously sought to challenge the hierarchy's traditional enlistment in America's military efforts. (Supporting the Spanish-American war, in a typical example, a joint statement of the hierarchy declared, "We, the members of the Catholic Church, are true Americans, and as such are loyal to our country and our flag, and obedient in the highest degree to the supreme authority of the nation.")

Two of the three Catholic peace organizations that presently exist — other than the Catholic Worker itself — have their roots in the Catholic Worker.

The Catholic Peace Fellowship is the largest of these, and the most recently founded. Founded in 1964, three of its four co-chairmen have served as managing editor of *The Catholic Worker* (Tom Cornell, Marty Corbin, and myself; the other co-chairman, Father Philip Berrigan, a Josephite priest, has been an editorial contributor to the *Worker* for six years.

The CPF is the only Catholic peace group that is institutionally connected to non-Catholics, in that it is an affiliate of the predominantly protestant Fellowship of Reconciliation, which for five decades has been involved with civil liberties, the freedom movement, nonviolence and anti-war efforts.

It is surprising to recall how much hostility there was, only five years ago, to the idea of a Catholic peace organization being publicly connected to a largely Protestant membership. FOR Church Work Secretary, John Heidbrink, a Presbyterian minister, had first suggested the idea of a CPF in a letter to *The Catholic Worker*. As one *Worker* editor put it at the time, "All they want to do is use you!"

It was out of that discussion, around a linoleum-topped table on the ground floor of St. Joseph's House on Chrystie Street, that the American Pax Association was born, thereby becoming another Catholic Worker offspring. Because of financial difficulties, Pax has grown slowly, but has succeeded in issuing a valuable quarterly magazine, *Peace,* under the editorship of Eileen Egan, an executive of Catholic Relief Services and author of *The Works of Peace.* Pax has also observed an annual peace mass August 9 and sponsored an annual conference at the Catholic Worker Farm in Tivoli, New York, as well as conducted monthly meetings in a room above the Paraclete Book Store in Manhattan.

Possibly the most important contribution Pax has made occurred during the Vatican Council. Eileen Egan was among those active in a Rome peace lobby. Others involved in the effort to influence the bishops were Gordon Zahn, the sociologist, as sponsor of Pax and a founder of the Catholic Peace Fellowship, and James Douglass, a lay theologian who was also instrumental in founding the CPF.

The CPF has been somewhat less energetic in its efforts to influence the hierarchy, though it has twice petitioned the Pope, once with 10,000 names. Its Washington chapter made a valiant but unsuccessful effort to influence the American bishops in the fall of 1966, when the bishops gathered in Washington, D.C. In connection with that, the group placed an ad in *The National Catholic Reporter:*

When Is A

B I S H O P S '

meeting a

HAPP

EN

ING?

maybe when

Pentecost first occurred

maybe when John

> called a Council maybe when our Bishops
> show they are bothered by the same things we are
> The rightness of continuing massive civilian casualties
> in north and south Vietnam — the draft — conscientious
> objectors to unjust wars going to prison — plans for
> universal training — laws against showing love of enemy.
> As Christians and Americans these things bother us. We
> ask for some concern, some sharing of our difficulties.
> In the problem of war, we ask that the Bishops go as far
> as Paul VI and call for an immediate end of the fighting
> "even at the expense of some inconvenience or loss."

The brief statement concluded with a request that those concerned express themselves to their bishops and fast and pray while the Washington conference was in progress.

The bishops, however, issued a statement in support of the war. No mention was made of such other issues as conscientious objection to particular wars, conscription, or efforts to provide medical relief to areas of the world labeled "enemy" by the government.

The least spectacular aspect of the CPF's work has been its assistance to conscientious objectors, whose numbers have risen enormously in recent years. At the Catholic Worker in 1961, for example, we received three or four letters a month asking about conscientious objection. At the CPF we have now lost all track of the number of COs we see or hear from each week — seldom less than 50, often more than 100, at the CPF's national and New York offices; but how many are served by our offices in Detroit, Chicago, and San Francisco, we really don't know; and it is impossible to keep up with the chapters.

Countless others write simply for information: "I want to do a paper on conscientious objection for my religion class. Sister says only Quakers are excused from military service."

There is sometimes the task of public witness. After Cardinal Spellman told American GIs that the war in Vietnam was "a war for civilization" our New York membership, led by Random House editor Alice Mayhew, conducted a vigil in front of the Chancery office. Many CPF chapters have engaged in "beg-ins" for war victims in both North and South Vietnam, despite government efforts to impede aid to all parts of Vietnam save those "controlled" by the Saigon government. And there have been "meals of reconciliation" — meals of rice and tea coupled with readings and a collection for war victims.

Out of its concern for the victims of war, and as an expression of penance for America's predominant responsibility for the war in Vietnam, the CPF was active in helping the Fellowship of Reconciliation launch a national campaign to raise funds with which to purchase medical aid for use throughout Vietnam.

When it was revealed in *The National Catholic Reporter* and *The New York Times* that Catholic Relief Services, an agency of the U.S. bishops, had provided material assistance to members of the South Vietnamese Popular Forces, yet was refusing to assist war victims in North Vietnam, the CPF published a statement that triggered a controversy that continued for many months. Catholics were asked to withhold contributions to Catholic Relief Services and to send their money to Caritas Internationalis, the Vatican's relief-coordinating body that is providing material assistance to the North Vietnamese Red Cross as well as participating in relief efforts in the South.

Through much of 1967 spokesmen for CRS repeatedly defended its program of channeling up to half of its food and relief supplies to the South Vietnamese militia. But in early 1968, CRS quietly announced that the program had been discontinued.

Other CPF efforts, sometimes carried out jointly with FOR, have included the operation of a speakers' bureau (Archbishop Roberts toured the U.S. for three months under CPF/FOR sponsorship, generating much news when the Los Angeles archdiocese asked him not to honor speaking commitments in Southern California), a tape and film library, a publications program and production of a CPF Bulletin, now a bi-monthly.

The only Catholic peace group not tied in some way to the Catholic Worker is the Catholic Association for International Peace. Quite a few would contend that it is no peace group at all. Certainly it isn't part of any movement, and is very definitely not inclined toward pacifism. The war in Vietnam has enjoyed CAIP's tolerance, though uneasiness with the war has grown among the Association's membership. There is no full-time CAIP staff. Msgr. George Higgins, director of Social Action for the U.S. Catholic Conference, puts out a very useful monthly newsletter on the Association's behalf. And there is an annual convention, the proceedings of which are generally published afterward.

An overview is subject to certain inadequacies, this being no exception. Hardly mentioned here, for example, is the perceptible shift toward resistance in the Catholic peace movement, which has impelled a growing number to refuse cooperation with the draft — the burning of draft cards by Dave Miller and Tom Cornell, the imprisonment of Jim Wilson, Bob Gilliam, Dan and Phil Berrigan. What stands out in importance, however, is the fact that the Catholic peace movement in the U.S. is growing very rapidly and has in its ranks a tenacious and important minority of professionals, intellectuals, artists, working people, and housewives. If the world is given a lease on life, much of the credit will be theirs.

13. The European Church and the War

GARY MACEOIN

"ALL THINKING PEOPLE IN EUROPE ARE AGREED THAT United States policy in Vietnam is bankrupt," Enda McDonagh said. "It is on the way to making the 'free world' a myth," François Houtart said. "The futility of the Vietnam war outweighs anything to be gained from it," Michael Ramsey said, "and its continuation will cause world opinion to be hardened against America."

All three speakers know the United States intimately and are personally and by traditional commitment its devoted friends. Not one of them is French, and I am sure none is Communist. Yet this is how they spoke in the second half of 1967. And between them they reflect a broad spectrum of the thought of Christian churchmen in Europe. The first two are Roman Catholic priests, professor of moral theology at Maynooth College, Ireland, and of sociology at the University of Louvain, Belgium, respectively. The third is Anglican Archbishop of Canterbury.

I regard the Houtart testimony as of particular significance. It was given in a lecture on the theological implications of world development at the Canadian bishops centennial Congress on the Theology of the Renewal of the Church, at Toronto, August 1967. The comment drew a spontaneous response from the several hundred scholars present from both sides of the Atlantic. It was the one section of the 90-minute talk that provoked the staid audience to applause.

Having reminded his audience that peace is indissolubly

linked to development, that (in the words of Pope Paul VI) "development is the new name for peace," Father Houtart added:

> One war in particular symbolizes the current human drama, that of Vietnam. It is not only that the enormity of the material means used for destruction makes one think of what could be done with them in development — the United States alone spends there in a month the equivalent of all the aid in gifts and assistance of the entire developed world [to the entire underdeveloped world] in a year — but there is a deeper symbolism yet. Vietnam is becoming, whether we like it or not, the symbol of the battle of the underdeveloped against the developed, the poor against the rich, the oppressed against the oppressor; and it is on the way to making the "free world" a myth.

Here we have one of the most universally agreed judgments by Europeans on the real results of the steady escalation of the war by the United States, namely, that both its direct and indirect effects are disastrous.

The direct effect is to pulverize the social fabric of Vietnam which it purports to build up. The point was stressed by Federico Alessandrini, editorial chief of the semi-official Vatican daily, *L'Osservatore Romano,* as Ambassador Goldberg was arriving in Rome in July 1966, amidst anti-American demonstrations, to attempt on behalf of President Johnson to explain the recent escalations to the Italian leaders and to Pope Paul. "Public opinion is perplexed and confused by the American initiatives," Alessandrini wrote in the *Osservatore.* "If the bombings achieve their tactical objectives in Hanoi and Haiphong, they will simultaneously destroy American policy, and not only in Asia."

More frequently and more emphatically I found Europeans presenting this argument in the concrete form of describing Vietnam as the Ireland of Asia. "One constant of thousands of years of history," they point out, "is the cultural and political opposition by little Vietnam to absorption by her powerful neighbor. It is the same role that Ireland has millennially played vis-à-vis England, deviously, tortuously, confusingly, as alone the weak can hope to contest the strong, yet successfully. If you regard England as your enemy, do you destroy or build up Ireland? If you regard China as your enemy, do you destroy or build up Vietnam?"

The indirect effect of the American strategy, hinted at by Alessandrini when he said that its success would negate American policy in other parts of the world as well as in Asia, is precisely that spelled out by Houtart. It convinces the poor nations of Asia, Africa, and Latin America that the capitalist West, of which the United States is leader and symbol, still regards them as expendable pawns in its game of world domination.

This is an emotional projection with strong racial overtones. The problem, however, is that there is a solid and continuing substratum for the image. As it lives in the European mind today, it is fed by a recollection of the arguments in 1945 in defense of atom-bombing Japan, namely, that a thousand American (read *white*) lives were more important than a million Japanese (read *yellow*). It is fed by signs on latrine doors in Vietnam: "For round eyed personnel only." It is fed by eye-witness accounts of how we treat those "on our side" in the euphemistically named *pacification programs:*

> The Vietnamese woman ignored the crying baby in her arms. She stared in hatred as the American infantrymen with shotguns blasted away at chickens and ducks. Others shot a water buffalo and a pet dog. While her husband, father and young son were led away, the torch was put to the hut that contained the family belongings. The flame consumed everything — including the shrine of the family ancestors.

That particular report appeared in an American publication, *Christian Century* (8-23-67), but the American general public is thoroughly shielded from such unpleasant aspects of what is happening, a tribute perhaps to the deadening influence of universal noise in our electronic age but surely no accolade to our vaunted press freedom and press dedication to the facts. The public of Europe gets not only a far wider spectrum of opinion regarding the war in Vietnam but also a fuller briefing on the events. Much of the information that reaches them, like much that reaches us, is presented in a framework of opinion or prejudice. The difference is that there every kind of prejudice finds an outlet in the communications media, providing the data for the intelligent man to make his own construction.

The belief is widespread and carefully cultivated in the United States that anti-American feeling on Vietnam is almost exclusively a French phenomenon, with the comforting deduction that it represents mainly the rantings of the bitter old megalomaniac who has been France's cross and dictator for years beyond recall. French attitudes, according to this theory, are hardened by bitterness at the U.S. refusal in the 1950s to support France effectively in Indo-China and later in Algeria, as well as by the jealousy of the once-great who see their role as a world power taken over by an upstart.

That such factors are at work in France and elsewhere in Europe (including Britain) is unquestionable. Nor are they the only complicating ones. The French do not like U.S. cultural expansionism, the so-called "coca-colonization" of Europe. Still less do they like the rapid increase in recent years of U.S. control of French industry and commerce, a major cause of the "gold flow" from the United States, and a major diversion of investment from the underdeveloped world, which needs it, to an area where it causes distortions but where it makes bigger profits.

These factors exist but they are secondary. The average Frenchman is only superficially and ephemerally anti-American, while deep down he is a friend for reasons that range from Lafayette and a common tradition of political liberty to the tourist dollar. And if he is more aware of Vietnam than other Europeans, there is the good objective reason that he knows more about that country and feels a historical commitment to it, a commitment sealed in the blood of his relatives and friends.

There is in fact nowhere more discussion, judgment, and condemnation of the Vietnam war than in France. This is something that transcends attitudes to de Gaulle. Not a single political party or journal of importance supports the U.S. role.

A 1967 survey by the Institute of Public Opinion showed a mere 10 percent as approving American policy, with 42 percent disapproving, and a high level of skepticism among those without a definite opinion. A considerable majority of those who expressed an opinion did not even believe that we were sincerely seeking a peaceful solution.

Insofar as there is a conditioning factor for the French attitudes, it is not the experience of Vietnam itself but that of Algeria. What shocked the national conscience finally was the barbarity of the methods that the French Government was willing to use to achieve its ends. This led to the institutionalization in the *jeune résistance* of selective conscientious objection (as subsequently affirmed by Vatican II) and an underground apparatus to hide young men and smuggle them to safety abroad.

That movement was given moral support in 1960 by the Declaration of the 121, signed by Jean-Paul Sartre, Simone de Beauvoir, Simone Signoret, and other intellectuals. The same people later led the protest against Vietnam. The Billion Movement, started in October 1966 to raise a billion (old) francs, about $2 million, for the Red Cross of the Viet Cong, was sponsored by Sartre, de Beauvoir, Alfred Kastler (1966 Nobel prize for physics), Jacques Prevert, Vercors, and many priests and pastors. It was but one of a crop of committees, most of them started by leftists but supported by Frenchmen of all ideologies.

The reason for this closing of ranks was summed up in September 1967 by Yves Chabas, of the French Protestant journal *L'Illustré:*

> Here in Europe, even we who are not Communists cannot understand your obstinate pursuit of this war. You are destroying this little nation that you profess to be defending and protecting. To us you seem to be awash in a sea of ideological hysteria. . . . It is hard for us to recognize Christ in the rich dress of military and economic power. We would incline to see him rather in a Cassius Clay and in all whose conscience requires them to refuse military service, in the black man who is turned out of the white man's church, in the citizen of Cuba or the Dominican Republic who fights for

the independence of his country. . . . Messianism is always suspect. Is it too much to ask you to give up your claim of believing that anything that comes from you is good and works for the welfare of others? . . . Why do you want to play at being the world's policeman, the universal moralist?

If the Algerian debacle can be pinpointed as catalyst of French opinion on Vietnam, the Vatican Council's evaluation of modern warfare and conscientious objection served the same function in other European and non-European countries. The arguments of Archbishop Philip Hannan of New Orleans in November 1964, arguments backed by many of his U.S. colleagues, were read as telling the Council that the Catholic Church should adjust its teaching to conform to the practice of the United States Government. Such caesaro-papism has long gone out of style in Europe west of the Iron Curtain.

From that time, there has been a clear line of disapproval, clear even in the statements of the Holy See, which always practices extreme circumspection in its expressions. Here, for example, is what Pope Paul told a general audience on February 10, 1965, just when the whole world was asking itself to what extremes the U.S. policy of reprisals in North Vietnam would lead:

> We address ourselves in the name of all mankind to those who risk pushing events along extremely dangerous paths, to those who today are responsible for the safety and wellbeing of the peoples. We urge them to re-establish relations between states on reciprocal respect and confidence, on moral principles which are natural and accordingly Christian. We urge them to strengthen international institutions able to prevent appeals to force, and to use these institutions which command general respect in order to ensure loyal observance of agreements.

Europeans also gave significant stress to certain passages in Pope Paul's address to the United Nations in October 1965. Even more than his impassioned plea, "Never Again War!", they singled out his statement that "one cannot love while holding offensive arms . . . especially those terrible arms which modern science has given you." The reference at the time could be only to American arms, for the inevitable counter-escalation by the other side had scarce begun.

Cardinal Alfrink of Holland pursued the same theme in April 1966. As president of Pax Christi, he told the movement that it should go further than Vatican II in stressing the natural incompatibility between the gospel and war. Every act of violence is in some way an anomaly and a contradiction of the gospel teaching, he said. When one takes modern arms into account, "it is impossible to maintain the theory of a just war, because the employment of these arms is not proportional to the suffering they cause."

The international Catholic-inspired peace movement took its president's call seriously when it met at Bergamo, Italy, in October. It issued "a cry of alarm at the worsening of the international situation and the multiplication of violence in the whole world." It called for a de-escalation in Vietnam, starting with a cessation of bombing, and asked the whole world in a gesture of solidarity to join in rebuilding Vietnam.

Two months earlier, the head of the Vietnam Union of Buddhist Churches, Bonze Nhat Hanh, had made a deep and favorable impression by his talks during a tour of Western Europe sponsored by the International Committee of Conscience for Peace in Vietnam. He said that a great majority of Vietnam's Catholics (the minority consisting mainly of refugees from the North), while opposing Communism, sought peace and rejected military solutions. He praised Pope Paul's work for peace, and when the Pope received him in private audience, he urged that the Pope go to Hanoi and Saigon to plead for peace.

Protestant opinion in Europe was by this time equally polarized. In February 1966, a declaration of the Board of the World Council of Churches asked for suspension of the bombing of North Vietnam, the withdrawal of American troops, and peace negotiations with the Viet Cong. The Conference on Church and Society of the WCC (which has 214 Protestant and Orthodox member denominations) reaffirmed this declaration in July. It condemned "the massive and growing military presence in Vietnam," and said there could be "justification neither for the American presence nor for the bombings in the North and South."

In England about the same time, the British Methodist Conference by an overwhelming majority condemned the American bombings and urged the British Government to disassociate itself from U.S. policy. Archbishop Michael Ramsey of Canterbury expressed approval of the WCC initiatives. And in an open letter to Pope Paul in the *Manchester Guardian,* Brian Wicker said that the bombings were "a deliberate destruction of innocent human lives."

One who helped to define the WCC stand is its youth secretary, Albert van den Heuvel, a Dutch Reformed minister, a man who has traveled every continent widely, on both sides of the Iron Curtain. In mid-1966, shortly after returning from Vietnam, he summed up his conclusions:

> If the Christian family has any reality, then the essential task of the Church in the northern hemisphere is to listen to the Christian forces in Vietnam. Christians in Vietnam, as elsewhere, are divided on many issues, but they are agreed in preferring the conference table to the battlefield. Most Vietnamese Christians have a much better understanding of what the Viet Cong stand for than do the people who are allied with the United States in the Vietnam conflict. The first task of the Christian community today may be to make heard the dream of the Viet Cong as it is repeatedly stated by the Vietnamese forces. That dream is not, as is so often said in the United States, that they are people who hate and destroy. The Viet Cong have from the beginning been a national liberation movement which wants to rid the country of feudal powers and substitute a modern socialist state. Socialism does not necessarily mean Communism. Vietnam has been exceedingly afraid of China all through its existence. To presuppose that the withdrawal of American forces would bring Vietnam immediately into the power area of China is only a dream. There are Christians among the Viet Cong, and they feel that the Americans should get out and should not stop the development of an indigenous socialist society.

Placing the Vietnam war in a world perspective, Dr. van den Heuvel said it is only a symptom of a much greater disease, namely, of the social revolution involving Asia, Africa, and

Latin America as they struggle for a new and more human society:

> Were peace to come to Vietnam, the next day we could expect a war somewhere else on the borders of the *imperium* of the United States. We must cure the disease if we want to get rid of the symptoms, and this will become increasingly the issue of the next decade. We have examples in Rhodesia, Santo Domingo, and Indonesia. The whole continent of Latin America will never be at peace any more until it has found a new way of structuring its society.

Dr. van den Heuvel was particularly critical of the United States for its abandonment of its own deep traditions:

> The U.S. always supported those who wanted to determine their own destiny. It was a leader in the decolonization movement. Now it is close to doing the very opposite by preventing 30 million Vietnamese from determining their own fate. The reason is that nobody in the United States knows what Communism is about. Americans have set up a spook and called it Communism, and everything that has the same sheet over its head is called Communism. This is an exceedingly dangerous situation for the United States, and it can be battled not simply by protesting government measures — which again are only symptoms — but only by a larger educational process through which people will learn to live with very different kinds of Socialism and Communism.

Perhaps no one incident did more to unify European opinion than Cardinal Spellman's 1966 Christmas statements. They were reported and commented on by all the media of communications from Dublin to Moscow. The items specially singled out were the statement that Vietnam was "a war for the defense of civilization," that "any solution other than victory was inconceivable," and that the United States is "the Good Samaritan of all nations" (Saigon, Christmas Eve); that Americans were fighting in Vietnam "as soldiers of Christ" (Manila, Dec. 28); and that they were defending "the cause of civilization and the cause of God" (Lubic, Philippines, Dec. 29).

Bishop Schmitt of Metz expressed the universal consternation in an open letter published in his diocesan newspaper. How reconcile your views, he asked Cardinal Spellman, with the

Vatican II condemnation of the destruction of cities and regions with their inhabitants as "a crime against God and man"? How, at the moment the Pope is urging a negotiated peace, can you call for military victory? Similar reactions came from Italy, Algeria, Sweden, England, Belgium, and elsewhere, strengthened by public demonstrations.

At the height of this uproar, Cardinal Cardijn, founder of the Young Christian Workers, announced his support of a peace assembly in Brussels being organized by people of all shades of opinion. Its proclaimed purposes were to call for an immediate end to American bombing, withdrawal of American troops, self-determination for Vietnam, and an end to all indirect help for the Vietnam war by Belgium as a member of NATO.

Simultaneously, sixty-six professors of the Catholic University of Louvain issued an appeal in the Belgian press:

> The United States is carrying on in Vietnam a war which is a denial of the official principles of its policy, and which is conducted against the right of a people to build sovereignly a new society on juster bases, a war which is the horrible result of a system of international relations in which the Third World is assigned by the industrial nations a form of development conformable to the ideology and interests of the rich. Far from being a war for Christian principles, it is a prolongation of the traditional policy of hegemony of the great powers.

Such is the kind of thinking which has dominated the European intellectual and religious community during those years. It was expressed again, for example, at the *Pacem in Terris* conference at Geneva in June 1967 and at the meeting of the central committee of the World Council of Churches at Herakleion, Crete, two months later. The general verdict of the more than three hundred participants at Geneva was that the U.S. war policy in Vietnam was a mistake. Many speakers described the United States as "savage," "brutal," and "uncivilized." The WCC committee recalled the various previous WCC statements and reaffirmed almost unanimously that "the hardening of positions and continuing military escalation open an apparently endless vista of horror."

"The unconditional ending of the bombing would be a decisive step towards peace," wrote Archbishop Paul Gouyon, of Rennes, president of the French section of Pax Christi, in the October 1967 issue of the movement's magazine. "Christians cannot acquiesce in such methods," said Msgr. George Hüssler, director of German Catholic Aid. He had been in Hanoi on an aid mission some months earlier.

An extremely dramatic expression of world Catholic opinion emerged from the Congress of the Lay Apostolate, which assembled three thousand delegates from all the world in Rome in mid-October 1967. A resolution on peace in Vietnam, developed at the workshop on Peace and the World Community, failed for technical reasons (as did most of the resolutions that emerged from the eight workshops) to come to the floor. It was nevertheless clear to observers that it would have been overwhelmingly approved. It read in part:

> We demand in particular that an end be put to the war which is destroying the people of Vietnam and which is a major obstacle to development. We condemn the bombing and massacres of civilian populations. We demand . . . negotiations for cease fire to be initiated immediately . . . for this purpose the bombing of North Vietnam be immediately stopped . . . a rapid withdrawal of all foreign troops. We appeal . . . to all Christians to personally engage in the reconstruction task of Vietnam . . . [and] to the people of the United States . . . to persuade the Government . . . to take the initiative.

Although European opinion makers have noted with approval the emergence of a growing number of opponents to U.S. official policy on Vietnam in the United States, as well as the appearance of a few churchmen to challenge the monolithic stand of the U.S. Roman Catholic institution behind the government, it is the common belief in Europe that the United States world leadership is ended because of Vietnam. The reason is twofold: the bankruptcy of intelligence shown by the policy itself; and the *herrenvolk* attitude of treating all allies as satellites and dismissing their objections with contempt. "Perhaps a Marshall Plan for Southeast Asia, with no strings attached, would restore your tarnished image slightly, after you have openly admitted your tragic mistake and got the hell out," a seasoned observer commented to me. "The United States is big enough to be able to admit it was wrong. But, since President Kennedy's assassination, who is left with the statesmanship to cut strings?"

The Church in Vietnam

14. Catholics Under Ngo Dinh Diem

HARRY HAAS

THOUGH FEW SOUTH VIETNAMESE CATHOLICS AC-
tively opposed the appointment of Ngo Dinh Diem as prime
minister in 1954, thousands left the country for fear of what his
nomination would mean to the national and social aims of the
Viet Minh movement, which they had supported for a number
of years. Events in South Vietnam, especially after Diem became
president in 1955, must have convinced them they made the
right choice.

The 700,000 or more Catholics who left the North at the
time of the "temporary" division of their country, were strongly
influenced by Diem's rise to power. He did all he could to settle
the Northern refugees, and seldom in history has a refugee
scheme been carried out more effectively. A factor contributing
to the cohesion of the refugees was that the Catholics, who made
up the vast majority, were guided, in their original decision and
in their subsequent conduct, by their clergy. Moreover, when
they reached the South, they preserved their former social
patterns, which helped them achieve an amazingly rapid re-
habilitation. It also led to their isolation from the South
Vietnamese, and the effects of this are still being felt today.

The refugees were a great burden to Diem, but a great help
as well. They formed a solid core of militant anti-Communists,
committed to the defeat of Communism and the recapture of
their territory. Many joined Diem's army, and the high proportion of Catholics among the officers (some say 50 percent)
consisted mainly of Northerners who had won promotion in the

field.

Northerners also strengthened Diem's administration. Just as educated Catholics had been the mainstay of the French regime, so once again they occupied a high proportion of the administrative posts, and provided Diem with a capable and reliable executive body. Later, their uncritical support of the government gained them an unfavorable reputation, and many were ousted during the anti-Diem coup. Owing to their qualifications and connections, however, most are now either back in office or established in business or professional life.

From 1954-6 Diem struggled to unite the turbulent South. He had quite a job controlling the armed forces, and the armies of the great sects — Binh Xuen, Cao Dai and Hoa Hao — which had waged an almost independent war against the French, had to be defeated one by one. By the end of 1956 a superficial unity was achieved. Unfortunately, Diem's supporters had little esteem for the pacified sects, and when, after 1956, the precarious unity was shattered by a drive for social reform, it was remnants of the armies of the sects who were the first to take up arms again and start vendettas.

From 1956 on, tension got worse and clashes became more frequent. The attitude of Catholics to the growing guerrilla movement depended on several factors. Diem was without doubt an honest man, a patriot, a leader. He would have made a good, progressive, pre-war emperor. In a revolutionary situation, however, he lacked the vision and the skill to lead his people in the re-structuring of a traditional society. His power rested not on popular appeal, but on an efficient administration (the legacy of the French). A mandarin by temperament, he relied on decrees being executed from top to bottom by officials of his choice. The reliability of these men was more a matter of a common education, community and class, than of a common vision or ideal.

"Diemism" did of course have ardent and sincere followers, especially among educated Catholics. The clergy, in particular, supported him. But the link between government and Church was a strange one. Diem's brother, Bishop Ngo Dinh Thuc, who had occupied the see of Vinh Long for many years before Diem became president, was the patron of a "personalist" leadership training camp, which had priests on the staff and in the management. Many people looked on the camp's methods as a form of political indoctrination. Furthermore, when the French archbishop of Saigon voluntarily resigned so that a Vietnamese might succeed him, Diem pressed for his brother's appointment. Rome compromised by naming him archbishop of Hue. Diem meanwhile made the life of the new Saigon archbishop so impossible that he was replaced by Nguyen-van-Binh. Thuc was doubtless the ablest of the Vietnamese bishops, and forbade his priests to accept favors from the government led by his brother. He himself, on the other hand, indulged mightily in such favors, excusing himself by reference to the traditional privileges due to the head of a family.

Ironically, it was Diem's moderately progressive agricultural reforms that did more than anything to drive peasants into the guerrilla. The Viet Minh had controlled vast areas of the South while the French were still in power, and had distributed land to the peasants, who had formerly been the exploited tenants of absentee landlords. Diem returned this land to the former owners, and in many cases demanded that the peasants pay back rent! Naturally enough, this drove a lot of people to desperation.

Diem also destroyed the traditional (Confucian) system of village elections. Previously the headman had been chosen from among the elders. Diem saw this family style of government as a stumbling block to rapid modernization, and replaced it with officials appointed directly by the center. This was meant as a revolutionary step, but had the opposite effect. The appointees were out of touch with local customs and the closely knit family structure of the villages. Opposition grew into armed resistance, and where the guerrillas were organized there were outbreaks of violence.

In the urban areas there were other reasons for dissatisfaction. Much of it was simply resentment at the domination of one clan over the others. There was growing discontent at the nepotistic and discriminatory aspects of Diem's regime, and it became a standing joke that you could get on as long as you were from one of the three D's — the initial for the party, religion, and province of the Ngo family.

The repression of "Communists" also did a lot of harm. There had been a large number of Communists in the Viet Minh, and many had stayed in the South when the Viet Minh fighters and supporters had fled North in 1954. It is also true that the Viet Minh was a very mixed bag, and had included a number of Catholics. What horrified the local population (and Diem) was that non-Communists were twice — 1945-6 and 1954 — ruthlessly purged. This was not an isolated phenomenon, but part of a vicious cycle of reprisals that began when the French suppression of guerrillas was revenged by an equally savage attack on collaborators. Diem, when he returned to Vietnam, had been abroad for nearly two decades, and understood nothing about the Viet Minh except that it was responsible for terror campaigns against non-Communists. It was irrelevant to him whether Catholics had supported it or not. After order was established in the South, persecution of "Communists" grew into a real witch-hunt, and many Viet Minh supporters were forced underground.

The murder of village headmen, teachers, and government officials, increasingly reported after 1956, can only partly be traced to an organized Communist campaign. Armed groups of Hoa Hao and Cao Dai, rebellious peasants, disgruntled villagers and rival politicians all had an axe to grind. Relatives of Viet Minh supporters persecuted as "Communists" sought revenge, and their obvious victims were Diem's local representatives.

The escalation of terror and counter-terror reached a peak in 1959, with the promulgation of a decree that virtually left no hope of justice for "subversive elements." In the same year a congress of armed resistance groups was held, and in December 1960 the National Liberation Front was formed. At that stage, it was composed of various groups, with a powerful hard-core minority of Communists.

Catholics who had suffered from the persecution also joined, and they did so more willingly because the NLF was headed by

a non-Communist, had a Catholic priest on its central committee, and was mainly directed toward the overthrow of Diem.
These Catholics were of course all Southerners.

Another group in opposition — though it did not join the
NLF — was the Association of Catholic Intellectuals. This was
a viable instrument of intellectual resistance, backed by a strong
group of labor leaders. Although it was criticized by more
radical Catholics for sheltering under the protection of the
Church, its effectiveness was important enough to earn it the
close attention of the Security Service. Its weekly magazine
Song Dao had considerable influence both inside and outside the
Church. In the early sixties, as the Buddhists began to organize
nonviolent opposition to the Diem regime, they learned from
this magazine alone that there were progressive and ecumenical
forces at work among the Catholics.

The association was supported by a small number of intellectual Catholic clergy, who were against Diem because of the
increasing lack of liberty, the use of oppressive measures, and
the partisan nature of his government. As Catholics, they were
appalled at the absence of a social policy, and exposed the
Diemists for the empty rhetoricians they were. They invited
Pere Lebret O.P., a specialist in socio-economic planning, to
draw up a program of development for Vietnam, confident that
a Catholic president would be grateful for such practical aid.
Diem did not appreciate Lebret's line, and the program was
shelved. This was not surprising, as Lebret was in the tradition
of the French Dominicans, who since the days of Lacordaire
have been protagonists of the French Revolution. The Spanish
and Irish priests who had worked in the North were more of
the traditional scholastic bent, and had trained generations of
North Vietnamese clergy to defend the status quo.

In the long run, the whole Catholic community suffered from
the Diem regime. Church leaders and most of the clergy were
reproached for profiting from favors extended by a Catholic
president to his co-religionists. Although, in fact, relatively few
Catholics occupied high posts, the Catholic community was very
well organized, and could avail itself more readily than other

groups of government services. Certain fund-raising activities—
notably a campaign for the construction of a church of pil-
grimage to Our Lady in the Hue archdiocese — were launched
from government offices. Church leaders tended to see this as
a sign of government sympathy, and even imagined the
Buddhists agreed with it. In reality, it aroused aggressively
hostile feelings against the Church. The Association of Catholic
Intellectuals warned the Church of this, but the situation was
such that any criticism of the regime was immediately identified
by the Catholic community as "Communist." The archbishop
of Saigon, who was in a very difficult position, managed to keep
unity among Catholics by refusing to take up any political
position, but under the surface there was considerable bitterness
between groups.

When the Buddhists started their nonviolent resistance, they
got no sympathy from Catholics, despite the fact that they were
in no way connected with the NLF. The Northern refugees, in
particular, who had lived all their lives in a completely Catholic
environment, under the guidance of priests whose ideas on
Buddhism were medieval, had no way of assessing the purity of
the Buddhists' motives. It looked like a "Communist" plot, and
Buddhism, anyway, was "diabolical." It took the Vatican
Council to come up with a more positive approach to non-
Christian religions, and the old ideas still linger in Vietnam.

The *Song Dao* Catholics, on the other hand, welcomed the
Buddhist upheaval. Their relations with leading Buddhists im-
proved as both groups realized they had common goals: the
liberalization of the regime, freedom and justice, improvement
of the position of Buddhists (whose leaders had been regarded
with suspicion by the government), lessening of unjust Catholic
privileges, etc. The Buddhists were very sensitive to injustice.
Not that Diem had ever actually persecuted them, but they had
endured centuries of alienation under colonialism, and had
reached breaking-point. The role of Archbishop Thuc sym-
bolized all their grievances.

The *Song Dao* group was the only Catholic body that understood the specific problems and attitudes of the Buddhists, and

a mutual loyalty sprang up between them which has lasted until today. This meant that the Church's intolerance was to some extent atoned for. Its bland facade cracked, and a variety of opinions appeared among Catholics. The image of the Church as a powerful and power-hungry monolithic institution — an image it had gained through centuries of alliance with the secular thrust of Western colonialism — began to be blurred.

15. Catholics in North Vietnam

Harry Haas

LITTLE DETAILED INFORMATION IS AVAILABLE ABOUT the situation of Catholics in North Vietnam. But one thing is certain: their isolation is not simply due to the political system in power. As with the Church in many other Communist countries, Catholics in North Vietnam have been virtually written off by their fellows in the rest of the world.

There are two reasons for this. The first is the assumption that a Communist government will automatically paralyze, if not eliminate, its Number One enemy: the Church. This is an exaggeration of the Communist fear of Catholicism, and implies a certain fatalism on the part of Catholics. It puts too much faith in the Marxist dialectic, which posits that Communism is inevitable in all societies. People who hold this view are really subconscious Marxists.

The second reason is common to Catholics in both Communist and non-Communist countries. They are all too prone to adopt a black-and-white ideological attitude to the Communist-Catholic dichotomy, so that they become incapable of thinking in terms of people — Communist people and Catholic people — as Pope John encouraged them to do. This has led to an almost masochistic delight among Catholics over each new persecution of the Church.

Contacts with Catholics in East Germany, Poland and Cuba, and a careful study of their situation, leads to a more complex assessment of the problem. The first fact that emerges is that in no two countries has the confrontation of Catholicism and

Communism been the same. The second is that the actual situation of the Church in each country varies according to socio-economic, cultural, and political factors — particularly within the Church — and is not just a matter of abstract, idealized doctrinal differences. In other words, there is no such thing as a Catholic monolith. Thirdly, the Communist and Catholic worlds are both going through a period of profound change, which means one must be always prepared to accept new information.

The Church in North Vietnam is in many ways the same as the Church anywhere, but it has certain features which make it unique. Perhaps the most important of these is that it played an important role in the struggle of the Viet Minh against the Japanese. Catholics worked side by side with Communists, Socialists, Nationalists, and Buddhists in a common movement for national liberation. Similar united fronts were formed against the Nazis in Europe; but what makes Vietnam a special case is that the undisputed leader of the struggle was a Communist — Ho Chi Minh.

When the Japanese surrendered in 1945, Ho declared the country independent. His speech at that time was remarkable, combining as it did the ideas of the French Revolution, the American Declaration of Independence, and the Declaration of Human Rights. The Communist cadres then proceeded to eliminate their rivals and took control. Yet there was no direct persecution of the Church. Certainly, some of Ho's opponents were Catholics, and some undoubtedy opposed him on ideological grounds. But Catholics who had no political affiliations were ignored by the Communists, who were far more interested in preventing any challenge to their power.

When the French returned in force, the Viet Minh revived their armed resistance, and many Catholics joined them. The strength of their allegiance is perhaps best shown by the fact that when, in 1954, some 100,000 Vietnamese left the South for the North, several thousand of them were Catholics — members of the Viet Minh; five priests went with them. Anyone familiar with the anti-Nazi resistance in Europe will understand this; nationalism can bind the most diverse forces together in a common aim.

Another reason why Catholics were happy to join the Viet Minh was that political indoctrination was still at a rudimentary stage. It was not until 1955 that the North Vietnamese Communist Party really began to inculcate its ideas into the armed forces, which were mainly composed of unsophisticated patriots. In the same way, the Chinese Communists left it until after the defeat of Chiang Kai-shek to make their army a politically conscious body.

The Catholics who joined the Viet Minh were therefore unaware of how much it was dominated by Communists. Had they been, they might have kept their identity more, and contributed to the lessening of Communist power and the establishment of a more pluralistic system after victory was won. On the other hand, they could also have been eliminated as a political force.

The Catholics who did not join were mostly those who lived in totally Catholic villages, under the patriarchal leadership of their priests. These people, especially those in the country to the South of Hanoi, represented a rather anachronistic prolongation of medieval Christendom. Their horizon was the paddy field and the church spire; their vision did not extend beyond the priest, the parish, the diocese, and, of course, heaven.

When the Japanese surrendered, they left no administrative structure intact. Le Huu Tu, the bishop of Phat Diem, organized a Christian militia for the maintenance of order. It was led by Father Hoang Quynh, who has, until recently, been the political leader of the Catholic refugees in the South. When the time came to choose between the French and the Viet Minh, most Catholics chose the French. By now the Viet Minh was considered a Communist organization, and any collaboration with it would be suicidal. Ho Chi Minh invited Bishop Le Huu Tu to join his council. He accepted, for tactical reasons, suspecting that Ho's motives were also purely tactical. He eventually died in voluntary exile in Saigon; before his death, in May 1967, he expressed the view that any negotiations with the NLF would lead to the acceptance of it in a coalition, or at least to its presence as an opposition party. Rather than this, he said, he would prefer to see a mass exodus of South Vietnamese Catholics to America or Australia.

It is not hard to find reasons for the negative attitudes of such Church leaders. For one thing, the Communists had ousted their rivals from the Viet Minh in 1945-6. For another, news had come through of the ruthless treatment of missionaries, Catholics, and indigenous clergy by the Chinese Communists when they took over. Above all, there was the Cold War, the dread of Communism as a world-wide conspiracy. These people could not know that the persecution of Catholics was often more for political reasons than religious; nor was the example of Indonesia — where a tiny minority of Christians played a major part in the nation's struggle — yet available to them.

In 1954, the year of the great decision, the Catholics had three hundred days to make up their minds. Some 700,000 fled in a dramatic, well-organized exodus. The bishop of Bui Chu led the move in some dioceses, but on the whole it was the parish priests who decided. In many cases, the people took with them nothing more than church furnishings — crosses, statues, and bells.

Those who chose to leave were the educated Catholics, most of the clergy, and a large following of simple faithful. But many poor and uneducated rickshaw-pullers, craftsmen, peddlers, and workers remained in Hanoi. Catholics in coastal areas tended to migrate; those in regions remote from the capital tended to stay. Ease of transport was not the main factor, for in the Southern diocese of Vinh only 28 percent of the Catholics left. Four bishops — those of Phat Diem, Bui Chu, Hai Phong, and Bac Ninh — went South; but in Bui Chu and Phat Diem only half of the faithful followed them. It is clear that some decided to stay because of their allegiance to the Viet Minh, just as some Southern Catholics marched North for the same reason. But love of native soil and a strong bond with the ancestral tombs probably outweighed political or ideological motives.

Two bishops — those of Hanoi and Binh — tried hard to stop their clergy from going away. Bishop Trinh Nhu Khues of

Hanoi even threatened his priests with ecclesiastical discipline if they did not stay, and recalled those who were studying abroad; 70 percent of them disobeyed all the same, and went South. The bishop of Vinh was more successful, losing only 36 percent of his clergy. The bishops' concern not to lose their priests was undoubtedly based on a genuine feeling that pastoral work would suffer as a result of the exodus. This has proved to be the case. All in all, some 40 percent of the laity left, and 70 percent of the priests, leaving three hundred priests — many now old and feeble — to care for about 800,000 Catholics.

On the day of the armistice, Ho Chi Minh and his cabinet attended solemn high Mass in the cathedral of Hanoi. On July 14, 1955, a decree on religion was promulgated, defending freedom of belief and of worship, and leaving the Church with enough property to eke out a meager existence. The decree also left room for foreign missionaries, and declared allegiance to the Pope a private matter. This was very different from the treatment the Church received in China, where Catholics were compelled to break with Rome. No doubt Ho was being realistic, but the role of Catholics in the Viet Minh must have influenced his decision.

Socialization inevitably affected the Church. It was laid down that religion could only be taught in church buildings, that people would decide the income of the clergy and that the activities of the Church must be submitted to the state authorities for approval. Some Catholics accepted this procedure with a good grace, considering it the best available under the circumstances. Others remained suspicious about the ultimate aims of the government with regard to religion.

The over-all situation could have been much worse. Some missionaries died in prison during the war, and there was a certain amount of local harassment — whether because of persecution, the exigencies of war, or mere personal feuding it is difficult to say. But the seminaries functioned, the Catholic press was quite vigorous, and the people's personal piety was better than ever. Catholic schools were nationalized, but retained their religious staff.

Then two waves of social reform hit the country, and inevitably affected the Church. In the winter of 1955, there was a strict redistribution of land. Farmers in the Catholic areas were better organized and led than others, and put up some resistance, but the Church made no official protest, despite the loss of most of her land. In 1956, after harsh reprisals against resisting peasants, the ruling group suffered a split, and the Church was given a valuable breathing-space. She profited from this time to stage a great revival, partly helped by new developments in French theology and catechetics (there were still foreign missionaries in the country). A further government crackdown occurred in 1958. The Catholic press was nationalized, the foreign missionaries were expelled, religious personnel were taken out of the schools and at least one seminary was closed. Many bishops and priests were put under house arrest. These two periods of difficulty for the Church were both caused by the predominance in the Communist Party of the more radical, dogmatic, and pro-Chinese wing, represented by Ho Chi Minh.

Since 1954, there have been marked tensions within the Church over the socialist policy of the Communist government. In 1955, priests and laymen organized an Association of Patriotic Catholics, which continued the tradition of supporting the Viet Minh. This movement is not really comparable to the "Pax" groups in Czechoslovakia and Hungary, exclusively clerical groups which sprang up after the Communist takeover in a bid to salvage what they could. It is more like the group of clergy and laity in Cuba, who have persisted until now in their support for Castro's revolution. In both countries, the majority of the bishops and clergy have remained suspicious — not without reason — of the tactics of the Communists. Those Catholics who support the revolution, however, remain loyal to the government, without accepting the atheism of Marxism and Leninism.

In North Vietnam, unpleasant incidents occurred within the Church as a result of some "patriotic" priests' voicing their opinions without the consent — and sometimes against the wishes — of the bishops. The hierarchy, as a whole, tended to concentrate more and more on developing the piety of the Catholic community, instead of supporting the forceful minority of priests and laymen who wished to contribute actively to the reconstruction of their devastated country and the desperate fight for survival. In those days, of course, there was no such thing as a dialogue between Christians and Marxists. The rejection by Popes Pius XI and XII of "atheistic Communism" had reinforced the basic mistrust that Church leaders felt towards the Communists, a mistrust that had grown with the waves of collectivism and socialization. Another major obstacle to any positive policy of cooperation was the "mission mentality." Catholics too easily assumed that anything that threatened their traditional mission institutions was a threat to the faith itself. This defensive and introverted attitude is common to most mission countries, and in some places it is far worse than in North Vietnam today.

In 1960, the foreign missionaries were expelled, and news became scarce. No North Vietnamese bishops took part in the Council in Rome. Most of the seminaries, partly for financial reasons (nationalization, the loss of foreign aid, the exodus of the wealthy Catholics to the South), but mainly for lack of staff, had to be closed. The life of the Church, however, was not checked. From all accounts, it has flourished, and loyalty to the Pope is strong. The only functioning seminaries are in Vinh, and few new priests are being ordained; but hundreds of full-time lay catechists and many women's groups have shored up the structure of the Church and compensated for the loss of clergy. Unfortunately, the continued isolation of the Church in North Vietnam means that the recent renewal brought about by the Vatican Council, which has offered alternatives to the classical seminary system, has not penetrated. Even if it had, it would be slow to be applied; for it seems to be a general rule that Catholic communities in Communist countries tend to cling to the traditional ways, as if afraid of losing everything.

The young generation of Catholics is undoubtedly inhibited in its adherence to the faith. It is still too soon to know how deeply the young people are being affected by the Marxism-

Leninism taught in schools, youth movements, and civic organizations. One gets the impression that there is a kind of co-existence allowed — a practical commitment to social reform and a spiritual devotion to the Church. Young Catholics do not seem to have been forced yet to rethink their faith in terms of Marxist doctrine, nor have they begun to interpret Marxism in the light of Christianity. Even allowing for the lack of intellectual talent among the Catholic community, a prolonged symbiosis of Marxist and Christian strains must result in some sort of cross-breeding. In this case, the Catholic strain would probably be the weaker partner.

Reliable reports from the Patriotic Catholic group indicate that the war in the South, and particularly the American bombing of the North, have done more than anything to draw the Church together. They are all North Vietnamese, after all, and nationalism is rampant. The war is a national effort, a heroic struggle to defeat the "American aggressors." Added to this, a large number of churches, several convents and at least one seminary have been bombed.

The Northern Catholics are well aware of the peace moves made by Pope Paul. In addition they share the universal admiration for Pope John. On the other hand, they also know about the late Cardinal Spellman's attitude to the war, and they have criticized Pope Paul for not having rebuked him strongly enough. They feel the Pope is not well informed, for he campaigns for peace without at the same time naming the Americans as aggressors. Perhaps it is they themselves who are ill informed. Nevertheless, the main thing is that they learn of every Catholic protest against the war, and they receive such news gladly. This will strengthen their position in the country, and may even result in more profound reflection on the role of Christians in society. It could also help them to break out of their isolation.

Nationalism in itself is not enough; it does not necessarily stimulate renewal in the Church. Catholics of North Vietnam will have to go further, building on the unity they now have and their growing good favor with the government, to become the leaven they should be. This is the only way the spirit of Christ can make an authentic impact on a nation under Communist rule. Nothing could be more detrimental, in this respect, than for Christians in the world outside Vietnam to dismiss their Vietnamese brothers as lost. On the one hand, they must acknowledge the Church in Vietnam as very much alive; on the other, they must do all in their power to pursue the dialogue with Communism, giving praise where praise is due, and criticizing where there are faults.

16. South Vietnam's Catholics and the War

HARRY HAAS

OVER THE PAST 350 YEARS ROMAN CATHOLICISM HAS sunk deep roots in Vietnam. Ten percent of the South Vietnamese are Catholics — a proportion higher than that in any other Asian country except the Philippines. The Church has an indigenous clergy, a history studded with the names of thousands of martyrs, a community drawn from every level of society. Yet in some ways still alien to Vietnamese culture, it exhibits many of the features of a ghetto church. And today deep rifts divide the Catholic community in South Vietnam — rifts which widen with each American escalation of the conflict.

The main weakness of Vietnamese Catholicism lies in its isolation from the people as a whole, in its independence, its aloofness. Its strength stems from a dedicated clergy, an unusually broad base made up of the devout and faithful, a sense of family-style community, a high degree of organization, and an astonishingly large proportion of educated laymen (an estimated 30 percent of Vietnamese intellectuals and perhaps half of the army officers are Catholics).

It is, however, not only in number and effectiveness of members that Vietnamese Catholicism is strong. With its hierarchical structure and its network of parishes and dioceses, the Church is the only well-organized denominational body in the whole country. Especially at this time, with Vietnam so desperately in need of help, it can avail itself of funds and expert personnel from Catholic organizations throughout the world. This advantage gives it a unique position of privilege and power.

Nor is the Catholic community a totally isolated, egocentric, politically united island within South Vietnam. At present its leaders (usually the clergy) provide the only viable means of channeling aid to the war-stricken population in many parts of the countryside. This is particularly true in areas where the alternation of political and military power — the government by day, the National Liberation Front by night — prevents the government's administrative cadres from functioning properly, if they function at all.

The Church's personnel are even more indispensable in areas completely dominated by the NLF. The Catholic priest not only stays with his own flock; he also serves the entire local and regional community, enjoying the respect and confidence of the people. Though he knows full well who has power, who actively supports the NLF, he rarely takes sides, considering his role a pastoral, not a partisan, one. This does not prevent him from having his own opinion and his own preference, and there must be many awkward moments. But in general it can be said that in the countryside the clergy do not involve themselves in politics any more than do the peasants, who maintain their traditional fatalistic attitude to the political vicissitudes of the moment.

On the other hand, the former refugees from North Vietnam, who make up some 60 percent of the Catholic community in the South, *do* play a definitely political role. In fact, they form the strongest united political organ in the country. In urban areas, particularly in Saigon, their strength is greater than that of all other groups put together. Their political competence was revealed in the recent senate elections, in which Catholics won 30 percent of the seats. Furthermore, the presence of Northern Catholics in the army, particularly in the officer corps and in the special forces, makes them doubly influential there. President Nguyen Van Thieu comes from their ranks as do many top army and administrative personnel.

The clergy who organized the exodus of Catholics from North Vietnam and played a leading part in the resettlement now hold positions of great social and political importance in the South.

Despite a shift from clerical to lay leadership in the government, no Catholic politician can be sure of support from the Northern Catholics unless he wins clerical recommendation. Most of the former refugees, while literate, are not educated, and they rely on their pastors for political direction.

This unity has often been most effective. It was street demonstrations by Northern Catholics which toppled the civilian government of Quat in Saigon; he had been suspected of fostering anti-Catholic legislation. The Northern Catholics also demonstrated their strength in Danang, where they first supported the Buddhists in the drive for a legal civilian government, then suddenly broke the alliance because they had begun to fear that a complete Buddhist victory might lead to peace talks.

The former refugees have always contended that the war is the result of aggression from the North. They are convinced that the Viet Cong is an instrument of Hanoi, pointing out that its name, which means "Vietnamese Communists," is apt. They are sure that negotiations with or recognition of the NLF would result only in a repetition of the 1955 and 1956 purges of non-Communists. Having sacrificed so much to flee from expectation of Communist horrors in the North, they can hardly be expected to display any other attitude.

The Northern Vietnamese Catholics were quite unprepared for the peace moves by Pope Paul VI, whose predecessors had long taught them to have no truck with "atheistic Communism." They had heard about such events as the Hungarian uprising, but more recent developments, such as Vatican Council II and Pope John XXIII's *Pacem in Terris,* had yet to make themselves felt. Only one Catholic paper in Saigon published news of Pope Paul's appeal for peace addressed to the presidents of North and South Vietnam, to the United States, the Soviet Union, and China. And even that paper carefully buried the story in the center pages, giving front-page prominence in that issue to Barry Goldwater's suggestion that China be threatened with nuclear attack.

In October 1966 Pope Paul sent one of his most skilled diplomats, Nuncio Sergei Pignedoli of Ottawa, to South Viet-

nam, hoping to unite the bishops behind a joint statement supporting peace through negotiations. Though too loyal as
Catholics to oppose the Vatican openly, the bishops considered
the *nuncio* misinformed and regretted his intervention. When
faculty members of Catholic Louvain University in Belgium
early in 1967 published a statement opposing the American
presence in Vietnam and a Brussels meeting sponsored by
Cardinal Cardijn drew up a similar declaration, the Northern
Catholics in Saigon accused the Belgians of "joining hands with
the Communists." In their telegram conveying that accusation
they pointedly preceded their signatures by the word *Veritas* in
contrast to the *Pax* used by the Belgians.

This attitude is of course not confined to the former refugees
from the North. Many Southern Catholics, faced by the growing
power of Communists within the NLF and worried by the
mounting role played in the conflict by troops from North
Vietnam, fear that any peace agreement resulting in neutraliza-
tion of the country would lead inevitably to total Communist
control. Nevertheless, most educated Southern Catholics — and
Northerners as well — stand in the center politically. It is not
uncommon for those who so stand to have personal contacts
both with Catholics in top government posts *and* with Catholics
in the NLF. Those who work for the government often regard
that government with a critical eye and refrain from identifying
themselves completely with it. They object to its overdependence
on American strength and to its preference for military over
social solutions.

Attitudes to the NLF are more subtle. Many Catholics have
at one time or another been involved in its program. They
know it was anti-Diem in origin and they cannot help admiring
its nationalist aims. With the growth of Communist and North
Vietnamese influence, however, many are becoming wary of too
close identification with it. Perhaps if the NLF had a leader as
charismatic as was Ho Chi Minh in his relation to the old
Viet Minh it would win more supporters from among the
Catholics. At the moment there is no one to fill such a role.
On the other hand, the Catholics know that the rank-and-file

members of the NLF joined the organization for nationalistic, not ideological, reasons. They point out that its pluralistic nature would be a factor operating against total Communist control if Vietnam were to be neutralized. In this dilemma they elect to retain their own opinions and their contacts. They refrain from campaigning for any clear-cut political solutions, preferring to feel the pulse of the hour and to exert what influence they possess to keep communications open on all sides.

On January 1, 1966, in the dark hours of escalation, eleven priests published a statement that shocked the public. They insisted that practically any solution would be preferable to the slaughter, misery, and immorality that the war was inflicting on the people of Vietnam. They even suggested that if peace should result in a Communist regime, the faith would survive. Since the priests who issued the statement were well known for their hard work among the people, they were not officially rebuked by the Church in spite of the extreme nature of their proposals. In fact, the sentiments they uttered are shared by many intelligent Catholics — at least in their more desperate moments.

Although the political center is the position that prevails among Saigon's Catholic intellectuals, one small group is to be found on the left. Its members spoke out fearlessly against Diem in spite of his Catholic prominence, and they persist in demanding a negotiated peace. The government censor is hard on their influential weekly, *Song Dao,* sometimes removing whole articles from its pages — in which cases the editors leave blank spaces as a form of protest.

Despite such divisions within the Catholic community, a common faith, the wise pastoral guidance of the bishops, and a strong loyalty have tended to keep the Church united. Early in 1967 the tension between right and left was heightened — on the one hand by the call for total war and ultimate victory, on the other by the demand for negotiations and peace. Gradually, however, the very fruitlessness of U.S. attempts to suppress the NLF and to stop Northern infiltration operated to provide a common ground for Catholics with different views.

In 1967 a significant article appeared in *Song Dao*. It was written by Fr. Hoang Quynh, who until 1954 had been the leader of the Christian militia in the North and who later had been the political leader of the refugees in the South. Though the article had been heavily censored, its gist was clear: a call for peace, for self-determination, and for cooperation among all religious groups, particularly between Catholics and Buddhists.

Behind this proposition lay growing awareness that victory was no longer a viable possibility. American escalation had actually resulted in a counter-escalation of nationalism, in an increase in pride — even among its enemies — in the NLF's heroic resistance to the American war machine. People who were well known as opponents of Diem in former days were now heard to complain that not even he would have permitted such an overwhelming American presence to continue.

Added to the growing uneasiness over the American presence, over the visible deterioration of Vietnamese culture and traditional values and over the low esteem in which the Thieu/Ky government is held has been embarrassment over the attention being given to Vietnam by the rest of the Roman Catholic world. Obviously the South Vietnamese bishops could not afford to continue to show themselves less concerned over the situation than their brother bishops from so many countries. Still less could they afford to ignore the insistent, almost monotonous, pleas from Pope Paul.

Thus it was surprising only to the most cynical that on January 7, 1968, the Bishops Conference of South Vietnam issued an urgent appeal for an end to the war (cease bombing the North, stop sending arms and other war *matériel* into the South). Nor was there surprise that the bishops, in barely veiled terms, criticized the present Saigon government.

There was little in the bishops' statement that was new. It urged Christians to live austerely and to avoid excesses during the approaching Tet festival; it instructed priests to organize a campaign of prayer and sacrifice for peace and to arrange conferences on the theme of the statement in all parishes; it invited "our fellow citizens of other religions to join their efforts to ours in quest for peace."

But what *was* new in the statement was what was significant. "How can we have peace," the bishops asked, "if those who are invested with responsibility — on no matter what level — content themselves with 'a false rhetoric of words,' if sloth, lying, cupidity, corruption and thievery are found in their actions? How can we have peace if the citizens no longer believe in their just cause and no longer have confidence in one another?"

Whether this declaration signals the fall of the Thieu/Ky government remains to be seen. It does, however, suggest that the hierarchy has departed from its public position of the past few years: avoiding direct comment on the political situation.

Particularly interesting was the bishops' willingness to quote, and to identify themselves with, the most quotable and dovish sections of recent statements by Pope Paul, including the famous "We cry to them in God's name to stop!" They quoted from the encyclical *Christi Matri Rosarii* issued in September 1966: "Men must come together and work out concrete plans and terms in all sincerity. A settlement should be reached now even at the expense of some inconvenience or loss; for it may have to be made later in the train of bitter slaughter and involve great loss." And again, from the Pope's address to Vietnamese pilgrims last May 24: "It is therefore necessary that the bombing over the territory of the North should cease and at the same time the infiltrations of arms and war *matériel* into the South should cease."

In effect, the Catholic bishops of South Vietnam were signing the Negotiation Now statement. One can only hope that they will have an effect on the mood of perplexity, even of despair, that grips so much of their country, and that the many Catholics in public office will strive harder to provide enlightened and nonsectarian leadership in the crucial months to come.

Afterword

A Protestant Reaction
by
ROBERT MCAFEE BROWN

A FULL PERSPECTIVE ON THE WAR IN VIETNAM IS going to be a long time in coming. Many churchmen seem to want that kind of perspective before they make judgments and decisions about the proper role of the Church in relation to Vietnam. And yet such a perspective is precisely the luxury we are denied. We cannot wait until later and then decide what we should have done. On the contrary, we are forced to make our decisions within the context of a highly ambiguous set of circumstances, without the absolute assurances we would like in order to be sure that we are being faithful to the gospel. Our decisions may in fact be a betrayal of the gospel, but the burden of Christian ethical decision is that we must always run that risk. And surely it is better to risk wrong decisions, which can always undergo the purging of public criticism and response, than to presume that we can avoid decisions, since the latter course of action not only represents a failure in the task of moral leadership but is also a vote of support for the status quo. Not to decide is to decide.

After reading the preceding essays and reflecting on what they say about American Catholics and the war in Vietnam, a number of reactions suggest themselves. I offer them without full development lest an interestingly long book become burdensomely so.

(1) Although the voices here speaking represent a minority within Roman Catholicism, they have become an increasingly articulate minority and they are gathering converts every day.

They can thus become the rallying point for an increasingly effective articulation of disapproval of our national policy. But having, quite properly, been self-consciously "Catholic" within the pages of this book, they will do a great service for the rest of us by not being too self-consciously "Catholic" in the future. There is scarcely a line in the entire book to which I cannot wholeheartedly subscribe, and yet I am not a Catholic but a Protestant. Many of the Jewish friends with whom I have made common cause in opposing our Vietnam policy would also be at home with most of the contents. Vietnam is not a distinctively "Catholic problem," but an "American problem," and from whatever theological base each of us proceeds, all of us must make common cause in the civic order in every way possible. Thus to the degree that this book becomes a rallying point for Catholics, I hope it can be a rallying point as well for Protestants, Jews, and "all men of good will," who are morally appalled by what has been done in Southeast Asia in the name of America.

(2) To the degree that the "official" voice of the American Catholic Church has been silent on the moral issues of Vietnam, it is of course appropriate that the primary voice of criticism should come from within the Catholic Church itself. It is not my task, as a Protestant, to lecture Catholic bishops about the appropriate fulfillment of their episcopal responsibilities — a truth I have learned the hard way after some over-zealous attempts in the past to do precisely that. And yet I would be less than honest if I did not give voice to the pain I have felt in the past three or four years, that (with a few brilliant exceptions) there have not been more forthright words from the American Catholic bishops about what seems to me the patent moral atrocity of our Administration's stand on Vietnam.

At the same time, and partly for this very reason, it is becoming clearer to me that all of us — Catholics, Protestants, Jews or whatever — may simply have to proceed on matters of grave moral concern in the future without waiting for, or expecting, our leaders to lead us. Pope Paul, to be sure, has spoken very forthrightly about Vietnam, but with the exception of about half a dozen American bishops, the American hierarchy has been unwilling to follow even him. And I am beginning to believe that it simply is not the nature of large ecclesiastical bodies to provide the cutting edge of prophetic leadership for the churches. I deeply regret this fact and wish it were not so, but there is much empirical evidence to support it. The large bodies have to be responsible to so many interests that they tend to be effectively muted even before they have opened their mouths. The prophets are more likely to be on the fringes of the Establishment if they are not indeed outside of it.

The solution, I believe, may be smaller *ad hoc* groups of concerned persons who come together transconfessionally around a single issue about which they feel strongly, and can therefore speak and act more forthrightly than is possible within the more formal structures to which they continue to give allegiance. On the issue of racism, the Southern Christian Leadership Conference is a case in point. On the issue of Vietnam, Clergy and Laymen Concerned About Vietnam is another, since it includes Protestants, Catholics and Jews on its advisory board, and is able to speak more forthrightly, and act more intensively, than any formal religious community in its own name is prepared to do.

(3) There are, nevertheless, specific things that American Catholics, and indeed the American Catholic hierarchy, could do. I am continually surprised by the unwillingness of the American Catholic Church to grapple in any official way with the problem of "selective conscientious objection." If ever there was a position made to order for Catholic theology to buttress, I would have thought this to be it. For regardless of how one interprets the doctrine of the "just war," it is clear that for at least fifteen centuries Catholic moral theology has been committed to the belief that some wars can be just, and that consequently other wars may be so unjust that a Catholic cannot participate in them. This outlaws any automatic "holy war" response, and it also underlines the fact that absolute pacifism need not be the only basis on which a Christian refuses to fight. The position says, quite simply, that Christians must discrim-

inate, and that it is entirely possible for a Christian to say that
he can participate in one war and refuse to participate in
another. Catholic theologians and bishops should be at the
forefront of a drive to have this position recognized as an
honorable alternative within the Selective Service system. They
are not. Nor are the rest of us. Because of our failure, the
young men of conscience who hold such a position will land in
jail. I hope the fact that the World Council of Churches, at its
fourth world assembly in Uppsala, Sweden, in July 1968, officially affirmed this position, and that a number of Protestant
denominations in America have done likewise, may provide a
slight ecumenical catalyst to Catholics to consider this responsibility once again.

(4) There is another area in which I would hope to hear
more voices raised within the American Catholic community.
This concerns the "4D" classification that is automatically given
to seminarians and ordained clergy, and that exempts them from
having to face the possibility of military service. Such individuals, who are constantly counseling people who face the
moral anguish of military service, never have to face the dilemma
themselves. Why they should receive this privileged preferential
treatment is far from clear. Societies that conscript men into the
armed forces have traditionally exempted three groups of people
— the blind, the insane, and the clergy. I have yet to hear a
convincing reason why clergy should not make their own decision about military service, rather than having it made for
them. If they believe in fighting, then let them go and fight. If
they do not believe in fighting, then let them face the same
crises as other men of draft age, deciding whether to appeal for
conscientious objector status, to refuse induction, to face imprisonment, and all the rest of the cruel choices their contemporaries face. Their total exemption from such decisions is
a privilege purchased at far too heavy a price. And since
individuals and institutions do not normally give up positions of
privilege voluntarily, here is a chance for a strong ecumenical
witness by *all* clergy that they will no longer avoid the full

range of human decisions that have so wracked the finest of our youth.

(5) The concerns thus far raised have focused on working within the system for a few changes. But I hope that American Catholics — and all other men with moral concerns — will be willing to pursue the logic that many young men of conscience have pursued, so that the Church can place itself more nearly at the forefront of moral concern in the future. That logic proceeds in the following fashion:

Vietnam confronts us as a moral horror of such magnitude that we cannot, under any circumstances, participate in it. But our perception of the wrongness of Vietnam forces us to confront another moral problem in our society, the draft, for it is the Selective Service system that forces one to go to Vietnam. Thus if the Vietnam war must be challenged the draft must likewise be challenged. In addition, the draft discriminates *de facto* against minority groups from the ghettos who have not had good enough schooling to get college deferments and thus avoid conscription the way middle-class white people do, it discriminates against those without sufficient sophistication to pursue a conscientious objector position, and it becomes the symbol of an increasingly totalitarian type of society that "channels" people into vocations *it* deems to be "in the national interest," rather than permitting individuals to make their own vocational decisions.

Thus moral concern that is initiated by the Vietnam conflict is likely to move on to a conviction that the draft itself is wrong and has no place in a democracy. Those who feel this way find themselves compelled to resist the draft, with all the penalties (up to 5 years in jail and up to $10,000 in fines) such an act entails.

But even this is not the end of the logic. For the more one reflects upon what Vietnam and the draft represent, the more one comes to see that they are not merely flaws in an otherwise ideal society, but that they are symptoms of a very sick society. Vietnam becomes a grotesque symbol of what that society does to its inhabitants elsewhere, whether in the threat of future

Vietnams in South America, for example, or in the ongoing destruction of personhood that takes place in the ghetto of every large American city. A nation that can easily spend $2½ billion a month destroying Vietnam, and cannot find the few billions necessary for restoring American cities (in implementation of the Kerner Commission Report) is a sick society indeed.

It is this radicalizing process that Vietnam has initiated in the hearts and minds of our youth, and there is a certain compelling logic to it that must force churchmen to ask far more penetrating and disturbing questions about the nature of our society than most of us have yet been willing to ask. Until we as a nation will pledge as much to development programs in the "third world" as we now pledge to sheer destructiveness in Southeast Asia, we need not be surprised if more and more of our most sensitive youth either "turn off" on the political process, or are led to increasingly radicalized forms of political activity. And since so much of this concern grows out of an extraordinary moral sensitivity to the inequities and dehumanizing processes of our society, do we not have a particular responsibility to support and uphold those individuals whose consciences force them to increasingly lonely and costly types of social protest? To the extent that the churches are the molders of conscience, those of us in the churches have no right to desert our youth in their hour of conscience.

(6) Finally, when we begin to gain any sort of perspective on the events that led up to and included Vietnam, we will realize that the story of the relationship of the American religious communities to the struggle will not be a flattering story. For all of us — Catholics, Protestants, Jews — it will be the familiar story of "too little, too late." We will be found to have condoned if not encouraged the systematic destruction of a tiny nation and its people, to have passed by on the other side while napalm was dropped on civilians, rice fields were destroyed, crops and forests were defoliated, cities were "destroyed in order to save them," military solutions were attempted to political problems, and mistrust and ill will to which we remained oblivious were mounting throughout the world.

At the very least, let us hope that some lessons will have been learned, so that we may profit by our mistakes and not be condemned to repeat them in the future. Some things we might hope to salvage from this tarnished era of our history will be the realization that (a) the Church must be the disturbing and interfering community, (b) prudence counts for less than justice, and justice must always be informed by love, (c) in this day and age the burden of proof must always be on those who *support* a war, (d) the unilateral intervention of great powers almost inevitably spells tragedy, and (e) the Church has a special vocation to espouse minority opinions and listen to the sensitive consciences of those outside her fold who may be the divinely appointed instruments to recall her to her proper business.